Praise for *Employee to Entrepreneur*

"I think this book will be of great interest to budding entrepreneurs. The authors write with passion and enable readers to understand the tremendous feeling of satisfaction gained from succeeding in business. I think the book has just the right blend of scholarship and practical advice."
Professor Peter Moizer, Dean, Leeds University Business School

"A must-read for anyone who is considering or has just started the journey from employee to entrepreneur – and a highly enjoyable one for those who are already on their way. Warm and wise, Chris and Catherine generously share their experience – good and bad – of starting, building and selling a business, with practical tips, good common sense and sharply observed insights. Perhaps the best advice they give is to remind us that being an entrepreneur is a choice and you have to make sure the choice is right for you and the life you want to live, not just the money you think you might make."
Andy Milligan, founder of The Caffeine Partnership, and author of *BOLD: How To Be Brave in Business And Win*

"Catherine and Chris were a pleasure to work with at UBEVCO. They describe the essential requirements of an entrepreneur as passion, self belief and experience. I agree with the first two. Experience is more the wisdom, treasured memories and learnings from the journey rather than a prerequisite."
Tony van Kralingen, Director of Supply Chain & Human Resources, SAB Miller plc

Employee to Entrepreneur

Employee to Entrepreneur

How to Ditch the Day Job and Start Your Own Business

Chris Garden and Catherine Blackburn

PEARSON

Harlow, England • London • New York • Boston • San Francisco • Toronto • Sydney • Auckland • Singapore • Hong Kong
Tokyo • Seoul • Taipei • New Delhi • Cape Town • São Paulo • Mexico City • Madrid • Amsterdam • Munich • Paris • Milan

Pearson Education Limited

Edinburgh Gate
Harlow CM20 2JE
Tel: +44 (0)1279 623623
Website: www.pearson.com/uk

First published 2013 (print and electronic)

ISBN: 978-1-4479-2958-1 (print)
978-0-273-77908-7 (PDF)
978-0-273-77909-4 (ePub)

British Library Cataloguing-in-Publication Data
A catalogue record for this book is available from the British Library

Library of Congress Cataloging-in-Publication Data
Garden, Chris.
Employee to entrepreneur : how to ditch the day job and start your own business / Chris Garden and Catherine Blackburn.
p. cm.
Includes bibliographical references and index.
ISBN 978-1-4479-2958-1 (print) -- ISBN 978-0-273-77908-7 (PDF) -- ISBN 978-0-273-77909-4 (ePub)
1. New business enterprises--Management. I. Blackburn, Catherine. II. Title.
HD62.5.G37 2013
658.1'1--dc23

2012040895

10 9 8 7 6 5 4 3 2 1
16 15 14 13 12

Illustrations by Two Associates
Cover design by Two Associates

Print edition typeset in 10/13 DIN OT by 3
Printed in Great Britain by Henry Ling Ltd., at the Dorset Press, Dorchester, Dorset
NOTE THAT ANY PAGE CROSS REFERENCES REFER TO THE PRINT EDITION

Contents

Acknowledgements

The inspiration for this book came from the ten incredible years developing and running Ubevco Distributors Ltd. We learnt a lot from a lot of people along the way.

Firstly, we must acknowledge the huge contribution of Dennis Miller, our partner in that venture. The core success of the business was centred on a close trinity. As equal partners, we were able to bring all the positives of being friends as well as our complementary business skills and experience. We built a business based on trusting each other, knowing we could depend on the others fully. Without Dennis, Ubevco would never have been born and it would never have succeeded. And we would not have anything to write about.

Our Ubevco journey brought us into contact with many people we should thank.

We had some incredible guys and girls working for us. They did a great job, showed real commitment and were powerful ambassadors for the business. They were also great fun and made going to work a pleasure. In particular, there is a small group of people who worked for us for most of the life of business who deserve medals for endurance.

Of course, we also employed our fair share of twits but we learnt some of the harder stuff trying to manage them so they too played their role in building our managerial skills.

We need to thank a number of businesses that entrusted their brands to us, especially Asia Pacific Breweries, Moctezuma and Cuauhtemoc Brewery, South African Breweries (SAB Miller) and the Red Bull Company. We were blessed to work with a small number of individuals from these organisations who treated us as partners and equals.

We would also like to thank our publishers Pearson for trusting us with our first attempt at writing a book. We would especially like to thank Nicole Eggleton for all her encouragement and elegant guidance down the right path.

Finally, of course, we thank our families for all their support over the years. As we dedicated ourselves to our business venture we did not always get the home balance right. Karen, Stephen, Kathryn and Jack all had to manage without us at times and yet still were there to muck in and help when called upon. Thank you!

Introduction

It was April Fool's Day 1996 when we started our business. Less than two weeks earlier our employer had appointed a receiver and we were made redundant. It seemed strangely appropriate to be starting a business on such a day given many would have considered it a foolhardy move in the circumstances. Yet it worked. Just over four years later we were turning over in excess of £100m and employed 130 people. And, still to this day, we celebrate April Fool's Day.

There is a lot of attention paid in the media to entrepreneurship these days. Often this focuses on young mavericks with innovative ideas and an eye for personal publicity, irrespective of whether they have proven financial success. The reality is somewhat different; the majority of new businesses are set up by people who are mid-career making the switch from employee to entrepreneur.

People like us in fact. We had an average age of 41 years and had spent over 50 years working for other people when we started Ubevco Distributors Ltd. In writing this book we aim to share the lessons we learned on the way to building our business. We will tackle the question of why and whether you should set up your own business and illustrate the real differences between working in an environment that you control and one where you are just a cog in a large corporate wheel.

The aims of the book

This book sets out to explain the benefits of implementing this significant mid-career change by moving from the status of employee to employer. We will encourage you to seriously consider whether making this change is right for you. We suggest how to do it in such a way as to provide a very satisfying career change financially, physically and emotionally and throughout we illustrate with our own experiences.

The messages we hope to deliver are:

1. *Experience is everything*. For anyone who has worked in successful organisations, the skills developed over time are strongly aligned to those you can use in a small business. If you look at *The Times* top 100 fastest growing small businesses, you will see a wealth of experience at the helm of these companies. These entrepreneurs have years of grounding in large organisations behind them.

   You can bring your corporate skills and the professional standards that often accompany them to a small environment where you can add the benefits of being fast, flexible and non-bureaucratic. This mix can allow you to compete alongside large and small organisations alike. However, you do need to be clear on your expertise and experience in order to be able to put them to best use and understand where you may need to find skills that you lack.
2. *Running your own business can give you real control of your life.* The world of employment has become increasingly uncertain over the last 10 years both through recession and the speed of technological change. Being your own boss will ensure that you are in control of your work life and can therefore plan for your future more realistically.
3. *It is easier than you think*. Compared to the complexity of a large company, managing a small business is much simpler. If you put in place simple and focused planning and organise yourself well, you will be able to make the key decisions to drive your business profitably.

We brought into our new company sales, marketing and financial experience, which was crucial to our success. The skills and experience developed in a corporate career, put into action in an environment that you control, is a central theme of the book. You can set the tone of the business, set the speed at which you operate and importantly focus its direction on meeting your long-term needs. We also developed new skills along the journey, most importantly the need to keep focused on the core business proposition.

We will highlight the advantages of working in a smaller company including the absence of politics, the simplicity of business aims and the gratification that comes with reacting to things quickly.

Who this book is for

We hope that many of the topics we discuss will apply to anyone starting a business, irrespective of scale and ambition. The focus though is on those individuals with a middle or senior management career within the corporate world, setting up a business. We will touch upon how businesses can be acquired through purchase or franchise licence, but our emphasis will be upon a start-up company.

You will be in good company. There are officially some 4.5 million private SME enterprises in the UK. A small medium enterprise (SME) is defined as any business hiring up to 249 persons. The majority are in fact enterprises run as sole traders without employees. However, there are still nearly 1.2m businesses employing less than 50 people and as a group pay the salaries of 10 million people in the UK. Over the last 10 years the number of SMEs has grown by over 30%, around a million extra businesses. In short, the figures demonstrate clearly that small businesses are a pivotal part of the UK economy and many experts predict rates of growth to increase alongside the technological revolution.

How we have set out the book

We have written the book in four parts, to reflect the various stages in the journey from employee to entrepreneur.

In Part 1 The reasons for going it alone, we examine why, when and what you might do if you are considering leaving corporate life. We also discuss managing this exit, whether you are doing it voluntarily or through redundancy.

We then move on in Part 2 to working through the practicalities of the start-up period, including how to brand your venture, minimise the risks and obtain support. By the end of Part 2, your business will have completed its formal Business Plan and be ready to trade.

Part 3 deals with the "nuts and bolts of running your business". Firstly, looking at the short term as you organise the operation and create your working environment. As the business begins to mature, we look at how to stay on track and manage your business relationships. Finally, we consider how best to manage growth and deal with change.

Lastly in Part 4 we share some less conventional lessons, situations and opinions that we came across during our tenure as business owners. These are not meant to be all encompassing, rather thought provoking, including some cautionary tales to be wary of.

Throughout the book we recount some of our actual experiences to illustrate the points of the chapter. These more personal recollections are presented in handwritten script.

Our story

Our story in many respects is not very unusual. We started out as work colleagues and ended up as best friends. This goes to prove two things: work can be a very fruitful place to find your business partners and it is possible to be friends and work together.

In 1996, we set up Ubevco Distributors Ltd with our business partner, Dennis Miller. We traded the business for 10 years after which our exit plan allowed us to retire with the accumulated profits.

We first met back in 1986. Dennis and Chris were both working at FCO, an advertising agency. Chris was the Finance Director whilst Dennis had a marketing background in the brewing industry and had joined the agency in an Account Director role. Catherine became a client when she joined Guinness with FCO as her ad agency.

We only worked together for about 18 months at that time before all going on to different jobs. But we stayed in touch. Dennis and Chris became good friends and golfing partners, eventually working together again at Maison Caurette. Dennis and Catherine became partners in life.

In 1993, after taking some time out from work with a young son, Catherine also joined the Maison Caurette Group. Whilst we all worked in different parts if the company, work once again united us and it was here for the first time that we contemplated going into business for ourselves.

Maison Caurette underwent a less than successful merger with another London drinks company, forming the Dolomore Group. The business owners (mainly financial institutions) were running out of patience that the company would generate the financial return they expected and decided the best option would be to break up the group. So we were offered the chance to purchase the beer agency business.

Before we had the chance to do the deal, the Dolomore Group went into receivership, putting an end to our deal and leaving us all redundant, with a statutory redundancy cheque amounting to a few hundred pounds each. We set up Ubevco on 1 April, 1996. Our earlier planning on the buy-out project had put us in good stead from the point of view of readiness. We were confident that there was a market opportunity for the business and that we could put the necessary finance in place. We had to draw on a lot of contacts for help to allow us to quickly put in place the logistics requirements.

Dennis took on the mantle of Managing Director and oversaw the sales function, Catherine became Marketing Director and Chris managed all the commercial functions including finance and logistics. As well as the three of us, we had two non-executive shareholders; both with financial investment backgrounds and we only had to invest £10,000 each to start the business. Finally, we invited 10 of our old colleagues to join us. As they too had been made redundant, they had nothing to lose and so we were operationally ready. With 10 employees and £50,000 in the bank, we started trading. The Mexican suppliers of Sol Lager had agreed to move their brand into the new business but we had more difficulty persuading the other agency brands given their experience with the Dolomore Group. However, Asia Pacific Breweries (APB) with Tiger Beer, South African Breweries (SAB) with Castle and Moosehead Breweries all eventually decided to give us some time to prove we were up to the task.

At the time, the decision for Dennis and Catherine to both be involved in the business did not seem especially risky. They had worked in the same business, albeit in different parts, for a couple of years and after all, were both out of work. Clearly, there was financial risk; both had to invest in the new company and derive an income from it. However, equally, both were confident that even if the venture did not succeed it would not have harmed their chances of furthering their respective careers elsewhere. So the risk versus the benefit offered by this opportunity seemed acceptable.

The first few weeks were very difficult – the receiver was unhelpful and maintaining enough supply to meet the demands of customers was a key priority. But as the weeks went by and we imported fresh stock the problems receded.

After a couple of months, we were offered the chance to take the Red Bull brand into the portfolio. Red Bull had set up its own company three years earlier and the infrastructure and advertising costs conspired to produce heavy losses, which the company was not keen to carry. It closed down the business and moved the brand into our business – strong proof that there was a place for our concept. We took on some of the Red Bull employees and they set up a small office in London from which they would oversee the brand marketing.

The next five years passed very quickly. All the beer brands showed healthy growth. We built an amazing team of people who were the source of great enjoyment and sometimes amusement for all of us.

Red Bull started to grow almost immediately and showed steady progress over the next two years. By the end of 1998, we had quadrupled the volume to around a million cases and then in 1999 we saw the volume shoot up to 5 million cases, over twice the budgeted volume. We had built up the team to around 50 people by this stage.

In many respects, this should have been the highlight. We were more successful and profitable than even our most optimistic plans. The big issue that we faced was the imbalance in the portfolio. Red Bull had gone from being the third largest brand to being the biggest and accounted for 85% of our volume.

The Red Bull brand was now more than big enough to sustain its own infrastructure. And whilst when it joined the portfolio it proved that our business model worked, it now highlighted the key flaw. The more successful we were in building the brands the point would come when they would be big enough to have their own UK operation.

But we were lucky and Red Bull waited another year before it decided to do so. By the time Red Bull announced its intention to go it alone in July 2001, we had increased the workforce to 130 and had turnover in excess of £105 million. But to be honest, we had had enough of working with Red Bull. It is hard to imagine being glad when you lose £90 million from your projected turnover but, in truth, running the business at that stage had lost much of its charm.

We had a very challenging five months as we restructured the business and transferred Red Bull and 60 of our people to the new Red Bull organisation. But our beer business was strong. We had just launched the Pilsner Urquell brand into the portfolio and after reducing our cost base we were confident that we were financially viable – just – to carry on.

And that is what we did for another five years. The joy returned as we had a better balanced business and a more manageable number of employees. We continued to see strong growth on all our beer brands and we still made a few mistakes along the way with a couple of new brands that didn't work. But the business model proved strong and we stayed profitable.

However, we began to discuss the longer term. We could not see ourselves doing the same thing for another 10 years. There were signs in the marketplace with worrying implications for our model as global consolidation of the major brewers moved ownership of brands into fewer hands. We felt that if we were to survive in the longer term we would need to strategically change direction and we questioned whether we had the energy and drive to do that. Our success so far had made us individually financially secure.

We agreed that the best course of action was to find an exit plan. After exploring all the options we decided to sell the business to APB who owned the Tiger beer brand. We worked with them on a plan whereby they effectively took over the business and the team. We were able to have an elegant exit from the business.

Final word

We believe there are many good lessons to take from our story.

- We had a strong business idea. There was a gap in the market that we filled.
- We had a very flexible financial model which served us well both through the periods of growth and when we needed to downsize quickly.
- We had a great culture that made it very enjoyable to go to work.

Overall, we could never have predicted the way the business would develop but we had enough experience to be able to manage the challenges as they came along. We had a fantastic time as owner managers and whilst we accept that we had a good dose of luck along the way we truly believe we worked for it and ultimately made the right decisions to capitalise on it.

It was the lessons we learned in our corporate life that underpinned everything we did and were the key to running a successful small business. In many ways, it represents the best grounding you can have to prepare you to be an entrepreneur. We hope that this read will be thought provoking and provide some help and inspiration should be you considering ditching the day job.

About us

Catherine Blackburn

Born and raised in Lancashire, I graduated from Sheffield Polytechnic in 1982 with a degree in business studies, after which I spent a very exciting decade working my way up the marketing ladder. I worked on some great brands with great companies including Unilever, Heinz, Guinness, Colgate Palmolive and Grant's of St James's wine division.

The draw of being a bigger fish in a smaller pond was strong. I joined Maison Caurette, a London drinks company, as Marketing Director in 1993 and started working with Dennis and Chris. Three years later we set up Ubevco Distributors Ltd.

As a managing partner at Ubevco, I enjoyed the challenges of running the ship and the following 12 years brought many new experiences that continued to broaden my horizons above and beyond my marketing background.

Since leaving the business in 2006, I have spent the last six years in a number of interesting ways. I took the opportunity to complete an MBA at Leeds University Business School; I had never found the time beforehand. I spend time as a volunteer with the Prince's Trust helping under-privileged young people. Finally, I could resist the call to work no longer and so set up Blackburn Garden Business Solutions with Chris Garden in 2010 with the aim of working with interesting companies on interesting projects.

Dennis and I were also partners outside of work for 18 years and we have a son, Jack, who is now 21 years old and studying at university. People often asked if it was difficult to work together and I could honestly answer 'no'! Dennis and I met through work and we have always shared an interest in business and the drinks industry. Whilst we no longer live together, we remain the best of friends. We both live near Dorking in Surrey.

Outside of working with Chris, I enjoy the freedom that I am now afforded to work less and spend my time more leisurely walking on the beautiful North Downs, interesting travel and time with precious family and friends.

Chris Garden

Born in Hull but raised mostly in Plymouth and south-east Cornwall, I graduated from Christ's College, Cambridge in 1978. With both parents and an elder sister all being teachers, it was imperative I did something different and so I trained as a chartered accountant with Touche Ross in London (now part of Deloitte). This was driven, however, by a desire to learn and experience business in general rather than become a career accountant. Upon qualification in 1982, I joined the US practice of Ernst and Young, based in the Cayman Islands, where with my teacher wife, Karen, we enjoyed a different experience.

Returning to the UK in 1984, I spent five years as finance director of a privately owned advertising agency and oversaw its sale to a fully quoted company. I then joined Maison Caurette following its highly geared purchase by venture capitalists and spent five years, first as Chief Financial Officer and later Chief Operating Officer, trying to stabilise this volatile but at times fast growing business.

Subsequently working with Catherine and Dennis Miller, we built solid relationships with international brands that were to stand us in good stead when circumstances suddenly presented an opportunity to set free our entrepreneurial leanings and resulted in our founding Ubevco in 1996.

After 10 great years, and the passing on of our Ubevco business baton to Tiger Beer UK, I was involved in some private investment initiatives and worked on improving my golf handicap before teaming up with Catherine once more in 2010 to offer our services and advice to other businesses.

One of the most pleasing aspects of my Ubevco experience is seeing how my son and daughter now use their experience of observing and occasionally helping the family business to help their own career development. It always sparks interest in the job interviews they have and the pride they show in it is very gratifying too.

Aside from all that, I enjoy all sport and particularly driving around the country watching Plymouth Argyle through thick and thin; well thin and thin is probably a better description!

Dennis Miller

Although not an author on this book, Dennis was a key part of our story, so we wanted to add the final point to the triangle here. Dennis is the third of the equal partners who ran Ubevco Distributors business. He has been fully retired since we stopped running Ubevco Distributors but he was integral to all the experience we gained from running the company.

Dennis was born and bred in Newcastle to a Geordie dad and Greek mum. His dad worked all his life for Colgate Palmolive, which clearly gave Dennis a taste for working on big brands. Dennis had a traditional corporate career in various sales and marketing roles with blue chip organisations such as Pedigree Pet Foods, Marks & Spencer, United Biscuits and Watney Mann Truman Brewers, where he became Brands Director, launching both Fosters and Budweiser in the UK.

His subsequent move into the advertising business is where he first worked directly with Chris and with Catherine as a client for the first time. We teamed up again in the London wholesaling group where Dennis was brought in to originally start up a dedicated operation launching Snapple before moving across to handle the beer agency division.

Dennis is enjoying his retirement in Surrey.

Blackburn Garden Business Solutions

Catherine and Chris now work together at Blackburn Garden Business Solutions offering independent business advice and mentoring in three key areas:

- small businesses aspiring to grow
- drinks businesses in the UK
- drinks businesses looking to launch in the UK.

www.blackburngarden.com

PART 1

THE REASONS FOR GOING IT ALONE

If you are reading this book, then to some extent you are harbouring thoughts about starting your own business. Whether you have been a victim of the recession or just feeling dissatisfied with your current job, you are at the very least intrigued by the prospect of starting your own company even if you have not yet made a commitment to do so.

In the first section of this book we are going to consider the issues you need to think about in order to take the decision to leave employment. We will consider:

- *Why do it?* It is important to really understand your motivations for embarking on the entrepreneurial route to ensure that they are consistent with those needed to succeed as a business owner.
- *When should you do it?* Choosing the right time to make the change to your employment status is a decision that faces every would-be entrepreneur.
- *Looking for inspiration.* If you want to go it alone, you need at this stage to have some idea about what your new business will be. We will look at how you can develop your ideas by drawing on your experiences past and present.
- *How you should do it?* Before you can move forward with your business start-up, there are things that you need to manage, not least of which is the exit from your current job whether you are choosing to leave or being made redundant.

At the end of this section, we envisage that you will have clarified your thinking about whether and when to commit to becoming an entrepreneur with a broad view of the type of business you may create.

Chapter 1

Why do it?

Running a business is not for everyone; for many the enjoyment of life in a corporate world steers them away from the go-it-alone alternative. Choosing the path of self-employment is a major change of career direction. In order to fully embrace the decision to change, you need to be very clear on your reasons for doing it.

If you have spent a good proportion of your career working in large organisations, this decision will be especially challenging. Everything about your environment will change. Large companies employ hundreds, if not thousands, of people across many functions and departments and sometimes locations around the world. In a small business, you may only have yourself for company and certainly will have many more jobs to do – who else is going to fix the printer?

Why consider leaving corporate life?

Thousands of people every year make the decision to start up their own company and the reasons behind the decision are many and varied and often very personal. There are four core reasons why people choose to make the change from corporate life. You will probably identify with at least one of them.

1 Dissatisfaction with corporate life

Every company you work for is different; structures, products sectors, cultures and personalities contribute to making each business unique. But there are some characteristics shared by large companies.

- Obviously, by definition they are big. This means that the distance between the top and bottom end of the power chain will be long and often the seat of power will be physically removed from the nuts and bolts of the organisation. This is especially true of public listed companies.
- The size of the organisation inevitably results in a fragmented structure broken down by departments to make organisation and decision-making possible.
- And for the same reason, to achieve effective management control, processes and approval systems are used to drive the functionality of the business.

As an employee, especially at junior levels of management, there are many benefits from working in such a company:

- career paths are available
- training and development opportunities
- great for your CV
- secure income
- benefits package
- good support functions allow you to concentrate on your job
- exciting product development
- professionals around you to learn from
- big budgets.

However, for many of us, over time the excitement begins to fade and the less glamorous face of corporate life emerges. This is probably triggered as we develop from the junior ranks into positions of responsibility and increasingly we come across:

- increased bureaucracy
- extended decision trees
- number crunching
- office politics
- feeling undervalued
- death of creativity as a result of the need for consensus
- limited opportunities to stretch yourself.

Big companies can sometimes go over the top in their demands of their employees – and the employees in turn can be too compliant. Many years ago our Mexican brewer friends had a European market manager based in London, and the story goes that they were concerned his well groomed moustache made him look "too Mexican" when dealing with the European market. They duly asked him to shave it off – which he did! Now it is quite possible that this story is somewhat apocryphal, but we can at least vouch that he did lose the moustache after many hirsute years!

A few years later he also made the journey from employee to entrepreneur – but perhaps this was just a coincidence!

Certainly though, the frustrations of being managed by the system as opposed to managing the system can leave us feeling disempowered and disengaged.

I started my marketing career working for Unilever and spent the next few years in the large marketing departments of Heinz, Guinness and Colgate Palmolive. All these roles served to build my experience and I had a great time along the way enjoying the perks that accompany working for organisations like these. However, as I progressed into middle management and became more involved in working on pan European and global projects, I began to feel frustrated.

I missed the sense of being able to really drive projects and take decisions quickly. The important issues and initiatives were often managed by committee. These roles were demanding but for the first time I questioned whether it was the sort of challenge that I enjoyed most. As a result, I made a deliberate change of career direction.

My next two jobs were in smaller organisations. They were not small companies but in a middle management position I had clear sight and contact with the senior management. I liked the idea of being a larger cog in a smaller wheel. These jobs still afforded me the chance to work on strong brands and progress up the marketing ladder but the company environment was very different. There was a stronger onus on taking responsibility for delivering at the bottom line, which I enjoyed. I was exposed to company goals and more involved in strategy at that level.

I certainly got more enjoyment and fulfilment from this improved sense of ownership of business issues and their resolution. This helped convince me to take up the opportunity to own and manage my own business when it presented itself a few years later.

Catherine

2 Job security

Once upon a time if you were good at your job, life in a large corporation offered the benefits of relatively certain employment with a happy ever after big fat pension ending. Alas, today such situations are purely mythical.

The business environment has changed dramatically over the last 20 years and today there are few jobs for life. The rate of business change has accelerated, through globalisation, mergers and technological advancements, and whilst this has conspired to create periods of strong economic growth it has also served to increase uncertainty in the workplace. Even outside of periods of recession the extent of business change has made a significant proportion of the population less certain of their job security.

Mergers, takeovers, cost cutting, downsizing, outsourcing, to name a few, are everyday reasons why large companies review their human resource and how to organise it. Job security is about more than just having a job. Even if you are not the victim of a reduction in headcount, you may find that your role has been changed and that you had little or no input to the decision. Being able to do the job you enjoy can be jeopardised by bigger decisions made up the hierarchy.

Sometimes, this decision is made for you. It is increasingly unlikely that you will make it through a corporate career without being made redundant at some point. Maybe at several points! Fortunately, the stigma of redundancy has receded somewhat as the scale of the issue has increased. Nevertheless it may in itself be a reason to leave corporate life for good.

3 Long-term goal to run your own business

If you have always harboured a desire to run your own company then the decision to leave your employment is likely to be an easier one. Your reasons are more focused on a positive ambition as opposed to dissatisfaction with your current situation. This does not mean that the decision is any easier. If you have a long-term ambition to run your own business you may well also have an idea of the sort of business you want and how you will do it. We will discuss this further in Chapter 3.

4 An opportunity

Finally, you may decide it is time to leave your corporate job because you are presented with an opportunity to move into business ownership. There could be many sources for such an opportunity from both inside and outside your field of expertise. In many respects, this is the best reason to leave corporate life as you already have the business idea. Yet, this option can give you the least time to consider the way ahead and care should be taken to ensure that adequate risk assessment of your position is undertaken.

The best reason to leave corporate life

All the above reasons for leaving the comfort of life in a large company are valid. But the best reason to run your own business is less about what you don't like about corporate life and more about the different opportunity that comes with being your own boss.

When you become your own boss you can take back control of your work life.

You will have the opportunity to create your own long-term vision for your work; planning when you work, how you will manage your earnings and ultimately an exit plan into retirement with much more control than if you are working for someone else. You will have the chance to improve the certainty in your future, increase the control over all aspects of your life and be able to properly plan for the long term.

In addition to these very tangible benefits, there are also many intangible benefits including the satisfaction of building a business, working according to your own principles and values, working with people you like and respect and perhaps most of all, the psychological advantage of not being reliant on any employer for your living.

It is a very compelling argument for starting a business. In your own organisation you will have the final say on every decision:

- your goals
- your strategy
- your financial plan
- how much you pay yourself
- how much you pay others
- you will decide if you need to upsize or downsize
- And you will have to decide how to get that printer fixed.

Running a business is unlikely to be a nine-to-five job and the early days are likely to be very demanding on your time and emotions. However, this will remain in your control and you do not need to conform to the myth that business start-ups will require you to make extreme forms of sacrifice to your personal life.

Overall, the benefits and rewards from making the move from employee to entrepreneur are great. If you make a success of your new venture then you can look forward to a great many benefits into the long term, including:

- job satisfaction
- financial control of your life
- the ability to plan your life longer term
- enjoying work.

You will be taking control of your destiny

Critical to your success as an entrepreneur is having a strong business idea and the means to execute it well. But equally critical is your personal motivation and mind-set. Without the right motivation you are unlikely to find the career satisfaction that you desire. If your motivation is only driven by the frustrations of corporate life, this is unlikely to be enough.

The right mind-set

In order to truly embrace the new world of business ownership, you need to be in the right frame of mind. Your mind-set will affect your ability to both make the right decisions and take the important next steps to move through the set up stages of the business.

The right mind-set is in part about being brave but it is certainly not about being gung ho. The right mind-set is about having personal confidence in your judgement and a determination to follow it. Without this, you will find running a business difficult.

In a corporate role your involvement in decision-making will be very different from running your own business. Key decisions in large organisations are likely to involve more than just you, sometimes a committee of people and often the need for ratification from above.

In a small business most decisions will fall to you. This is likely to be the biggest change you will experience and you need to be sure that you will both cope and perhaps more importantly enjoy this. It is not just the number of decisions that will change but also the scope of the decisions. You will need to face strategic decisions, financial decisions, practical decisions, emotional decisions, big decisions, and little decisions.

Be honest with yourself. If you are the one who likes to sit on the fence when decisions are needed, this may not be for you.

This issue is less about risk tolerance. The right mind-set is about confidence in yourself; understanding that your experience and judgement combine to great effect. There will be many times, especially early on, where you will be out of your comfort zone. You need to accept this and learn the difference between feeling out of your comfort zone and feeling that the decision is wrong.

With the right mind-set you will have the confidence to make decisions and the attitude to accept the outcome and move on. You will not always make the right decision but you can always move forward to the next with the confidence to make the best decision next time.

Like most things in life, your management of decisions will improve the more you practise it.

As the owner of a business, you have to be able to look on the bright side and see the way ahead as positive. Through Part 2 we will discuss the preparation you need to do to underpin this vision. Seeing the long-term goal should always guide the next short-term decision.

The success you have experienced in your career to date will be the result of you doing your job well and you will have accumulated a lot of business experience. The experience itself will be invaluable when you are managing your own company but equally important is the confidence that you should have in your own ability. This will give you the positive mind-set you need.

Over the course of the book we will offer some guidance on where and how you can help yourself when you face situations that are new to you or where you feel inexperienced.

There may be some good reasons why you may be feeling

indecisive right now. Your current employment situation may mean you are feeling less than positive. Recession increases instability many fold. Redundancy offers particular challenges over and above the obvious loss of income. Being made redundant does not mean we have failed somehow in our job and yet we will probably have faced an extended period of uncertainty as well as feeling physically and emotionally tired.

Obviously, your personal circumstances (especially the financial ones) can affect your immediate actions and we will cover this in Chapter 2. In Chapter 4 we will discuss some of the practical specifics of managing this situation. You may have the opportunity to take your time and fully review your options or you may need to take some urgent contingency action to secure short-term income.

Most importantly, this situation could offer you a unique opportunity to wrestle back some control in your life rather than be at the beck and call of your employer's fortunes within a roller coaster economy. This could be your opportunity to take control of your future working life.

If you are to embark on this journey, you need to start from the point where you believe you have the skills to do it and the experience to learn along the way where necessary. We will try in this book to help you on the way too.

In summary

There are many, many reasons why people choose to leave employment and embark upon an entrepreneurial venture:

- dissatisfaction with corporate life
- the need for job security
- a long-term desire to run a business
- a business opportunity presents itself.

Understanding your motivation is key to making the right decision. The change to your life will be very significant; you will experience increased risk both financially and to your lifestyle. You need to be sure that you are ready and able to manage the changes that will happen.

The essence of this book is to try to help you to decide if you are ready to make this change. Time and time again we will advise you to reflect back on the experience you have gained in your past work life and see that the decisions you have to make in your own business are often the same as you have made on many occasions for other companies.

If the challenge of having the responsibility for all the decisions excites you, then carry on reading. We aim to address all of the big questions you will face and give you some insight into how we managed our business in the same situation.

Chapter 2

When should you do it?

One of the most difficult decisions you will face is deciding on the right time to make your move. Even if you have already left your employment and have a ready-made business idea, it is quite likely that you will get an attack of nerves and be having second thoughts.

This is probably no different to experiences you have had before when switching jobs or even embarking upon your career in the first place. There is any number of reasons for deciding against moving forward with your plans, or at least delay them.

"Why I should delay starting:

- The economy is bad.
- It's the wrong season.
- Let's see if another job comes up that I fancy.
- My market conditions might be changing so let's see what happens first.
- Not a good time at home – wife/child/relations have big events looming."

It is easy to understand this kind of concern, but equally there are usually positives to take out of any negative situation. Take the recession that struck much of the Western world economy in 2008 and subsequent years. You would be mad to try and start a business in such a recession wouldn't you? Well not necessarily – let's consider the positive factors.

1. Business failures may have created gaps in the market for newer, leaner players to fill.
2. Prices are keener all round whether its office space, materials or whatever is vital to your particular business.
3. Interest rates are low making borrowing and financing your business cheaper.
4. There are more people available on the job market and they are cheaper than usual.
5. Buyers are under pressure to review and source the best supplier, so opportunities exist for more efficient operators like you!
6. Governments are offering help and incentives to encourage business start up and growth.

7 Succeeding through the recession suggests your business will then boom when the economy recovers.

Delaying tactics can often mean that you have broader doubts about leaving the employment world, and this is understandable. It is easy to compile a list of reasons why not to do it:

"Why I shouldn't do it:

- There's the mortgage to pay.
- Too much responsibility.
- Can I manage the hard work?
- Is it fair on my family?
- What if it fails?
- Will I go bankrupt?
- Can I ever go back to a corporate career?
- Am I blowing my redundancy package?
- I am too old.
- I don't know enough."

Concerns around the family are usually high on any list. Are you sacrificing your children's future on the back of an experiment? Will you have less time to spend with your children? How will you manage childcare provision if you are working longer hours? Clearly identifying the issues that affect the family is an important start point for you if you are to be able to properly assess this issue.

It is hard to criticise most of these reasons as valid concerns. For many people owning and running a business is just too risky. Nevertheless, addressing all concerns at this point can be a helpful and meaningful process – call it if you like the final risk assessment of your proposed move away from corporate life.

Risk assessment

For most people the primary concern and reservation will revolve around income. Can I earn a living? This will be particularly focused around the short term. Inevitably, your business will take time to start generating an income and cash flow is usually negative whilst you incur the costs of establishing your business infrastructure.

The best way of alleviating your concerns is to prepare both a personal and business budget, and plan how you can make it work. Take a pessimistic view on how long it might take for your business to produce sufficient cash flow for you to start drawing significant income, and then assess whether you can meet your personal obligations in the meantime.

We will be tackling the issue of the business budget in detail in Chapter 6. Preparing a personal budget is essentially a review of your household spending. You need to review all the costs that you (and your family) incur, including:

- mortgage
- household bills, including utility bills, food, clothing, etc.
- car and associated costs
- any other costs such as holidays, school fees, etc. which regularly feature in your spending.

Against these costs you need to identify all your sources of income, which can include:

- your income
- your spouse's income
- savings
- investments.

This will allow you to look radically at your options for balancing your personal budget in the short term as your income from employment is replaced by income from a new venture. As with a business budget, try to project your costs and income over a twelve-month period.

According to your circumstances, there may be a number of different ways you can fund these requirements. Establishing the amounts involved will help you work out how you personally can achieve it. If you have a plan, it will give you the confidence that this is not a reason to delay or cancel your starting up.

Potential sources of finance while you establish your business

These may include:

- the use of redundancy payments
- family savings
- family or friends' support
- maintaining existing employment whilst starting up
- other part-time employment
- your partner's earnings to support the family
- bank support e.g. overdraft facility, bank loans
- car sale or re-financing
- the release of funds from any personal spare assets
- mortgage holidays by arrangement with your lender
- local enterprise or community organisation
- seeking investment in your business from equity providers
- franchise loans.

Developing your personal plan might change your perspective on things. It may even lead you to seek an active partner to help finance the business, or a silent investor. It is very common to get help from family, friends, business colleagues or a business mentor and in return give them a small stake in your business or some other financial reward. We will return to the specific subject of mentors and financial backers in later chapters.

Your personal risk assessment should not be confined merely to short-term financial concerns. There are other issues that you should think about such as any health or relationship factors that might affect your ability to put in the hard graft needed to drive any new venture forward. By undertaking the process of considering all the risk scenarios, you will most often find potential solutions that are available if things do not go as well as you expected.

One of the great benefits of owning your own business is that it provides great flexibility. You can tailor how, where and when you conduct business to a large extent and this can usually overcome personal life complications. Achieving a better work–life balance and personal fulfilment are after all two of the key reasons why you want to escape life as a corporate employee. This is particularly important in addressing concerns about the family.

Much is published about the difficulties for women having to manage career and children. Being truly in charge of a business does not necessarily reduce the demands of the business but it at least offers two benefits: first you can choose when and sometimes where you work, and, secondly, you do not have a boss pressing the psychological guilt button. So at those really stressful times, such as when children are ill, you have the flexibility to avoid feeling you are letting either work or family (or both) down.

When my son Jack was about eight years old he was fed up with attending after-school club. In his eyes, having to stay at school after the end of the school day was tiresome. As we lived near the office, he attended a school close by; so, he and I agreed a compromise. He could come to the office after school as long as he agreed to do his homework and not disturb anyone else.

On the whole, this worked fine. It gave me longer at the office and when he did eventually get bored he usually did a few errands for people in the office and he acquired the job of re-stocking the office drinks fridge. Everyone knew him and he knew everyone – he was almost one of the team.

And in return, on a cold December day, everyone in the office would trail outside into the town pedestrian shopping area to listen to Jack's school carol singing. Mutual support!

Catherine

Remembering that it is not all about the money is an important step to overcoming any doubts. Your other motivations are more important: the freedom, enjoyment and enhanced status that you gain from running your own operation should drive you on and the financial rewards will follow too as you make a success of your new venture.

So having your fall back personal plan tucked away is in no way to be interpreted as a negative step, rather it is to give you added confidence in the viability of your decision, and demonstrates the thoroughness you need to be an accomplished business owner.

You may still have concerns about specific timing issues, and you hear lots of excuses:

- "Don't start a business in August because everyone is away on holiday."
- "Nobody is spending any money at the moment."
- "The competition have just invested in more advertising."

There are always some less than perfect market conditions, real or perceived to put one off starting something off. Our advice is to focus on your core strengths and positions of power.

Positions of power

It is highly unlikely that all the external factors that might help your business are all going to be favourable at the same time, but there will be some areas where you have some particular advantages – your own particular points of power. By focusing on these you will reach the conclusion that now is a perfectly good time to start your business. If you choose to delay for 12 months the factors that were previously unfavourable might now be favourable and vice versa. You will have a different set of positions of power and there will be another good time to start your business, probably not any better or worse in the long term than doing it now.

If you are going into business with partners, or perhaps buying a franchise, then things may be easier. You have the support network that your partners provide and you can share common concerns. Specific issues for one partner might be resolvable by another, especially if these concern personal factors and restraints. In the case of a franchise, they have the experience of managing all your start up issues and the benefit of historical performance to help give you confidence; remembering always that a franchisor is generally going to paint you a positive picture of prospects.

By reminding yourself of your strengths and having a clear plan to manage the risks involved, you should feel confident that there is no wrong time to get started, even if all your personal and business circumstances are not all in perfect alignment.

How we identified our positions of strength

For a number of months prior to our redundancy, we had believed that we would soon be shareholders of the Beer brand division bought out of our employer. The business would have had significant external funding and venture capital masters – but it would have come with the safety of all existing brand owner contracts and active customers, proper inventories, an existing infrastructure and active marketing programmes.

The situation we found ourselves in was entirely different. The Dolomore Group had gone into receivership before the deal had gone through. On the face of it, we only had the support so far of one product supplier, albeit it was the biggest one, with Sol and Dos Equis. We could not hope to build a stable business with just one brand. We would need to persuade other brands that we could start a new business and properly represent them with sufficient sales, marketing and logistical resource.

There is nothing like the repossession of your company car to put things into stark reality. When Catherine received a call from a headhunter, just minutes after they had removed her nice white BMW from her drive, she felt compelled to listen. 'Blue Chip Company, senior marketing position, good package, need someone quickly' it was all there. It seemed like a no brainer – new house with new mortgage, young child, and with both parents just been made redundant. Surely she needed that job.

Yet, it was not what Catherine really wanted. She had been looking forward to being able to manage a smaller business as part of a small executive management team and with a meaningful share of the ownership. The secure choice was to stay in employment, particularly as for Catherine and Dennis it was a 'double whammy', they were both planning to work in the same business, same risk but double the impact.

It was time to put up or shut up, and so the prospective business partners met over dinner to make that decision.

The more we ate and talked, the more we realised that we had many positions of strength.

Firstly, we had the ability to move quickly, maintaining supply, and much more quickly than any potential rival organisation could.

Secondly, we believed that we could put together a credible workforce. Many of the sales team that we had worked with were also being made redundant. There were some strong performers who covered the key trade sectors we needed. The receiver was only offering the minimal statutory redundancy that he was obliged to pay. So we supposed that most would take up any offer we made – at least to bide their time and look for other offers!

Thirdly, we were confident that we had the management expertise and determination to succeed.

Finally, we had a business plan that was realistic but cautious.

As we summarised our position, we realised it was a strong one. We could immediately offer continued supply of product which was good for our beer brand owners and their customers, and also to some of the old team, jobs. It bought everyone time – it gave us the time to demonstrate our new business could produce results for our clients and suppliers and gave the employees time to look at other options. As the new 'entrepreneurs' our business plan required us to only invest £10,000 each as extra capital in the business and whilst we would only earn a modest salary, it also gave us employment.

Whilst the timing in some ways could not have been worse from a personal aspect for Dennis and Catherine, a calm assessment of our positions of strength was persuasive. We had reached a decision. We would start trading.

There is never a wrong time

We know many friends and colleagues who have speculated as they near the end of their careers that they had thought about starting up on their own "but the timing wasn't right" usually followed by a justification of what held them back "Michael was just doing his GCSE's" or "We had only just moved house" or whatever.

You can always find a reason why it's the wrong time to leave your job and move in this new direction. In many ways the redundant worker is the lucky one – this gives a real opportunity and freedom to make the move into an entrepreneurial way of life. As we listed earlier there are lots of reasons for not starting up, but they can be easily refuted.

Why I shouldn't do it	Of course, you should
Mortgage to pay	Negotiate or re-finance
Too much responsibility	You will thrive on responsibility
Can I manage the hard work?	As owner, hard work is more rewarding
Is it fair on my family?	You can manage your own life/work balance
What if it fails?	Go back to being an employee
Will I go bankrupt?	Not with good planning
Can I go back to a corporate career?	If you have to, you probably can
Am I blowing my redundancy pay?	All investments carry some risk
I am too old	No
I don't know enough	Focus on strengths; get help with other things
My children will suffer	Choose a business that allows you to fit work around your children
Getting divorced	This is the incentive you need to go it alone

We firmly believe that there is never a wrong time provided that –

- you adopt the right mentality to become a business owner
- you are truly motivated to escape being a long term employee
- you have assessed your risk factors.

Of course, some occasions may be better than others in terms of both your personal circumstances and the specific state of the business and economy that you are going to be operating in. However, it is highly improbable that everything will be in perfect position for you to start up and if you wait for that to happen it probably never will.

Business heroes

Sometimes it is helpful to think about those people that have achieved already. There may be examples in your own field or maybe individuals that you can particularly relate to given their personal history, age, etc. Looking for inspiration from people who have already made it can be both instructive in terms of how they achieved and supportive in times of insecurity.

EXAMPLE *Dietrich Mateschitz, creator of the Red Bull brand*

Dietrich is a great example of a brilliant entrepreneur.

He had an established corporate marketing career working for Unilever and Blendax, a German cosmetics company now owned by Procter and Gamble. As part of his role with Blendax, he regularly travelled to the Far East. As he got off his early morning long-haul flight, he was intrigued by a drink used by taxi drivers to keep them awake. The product was called Krating Daeng, and Mateschitz found that it also helped with his jetlag.

In 1984, Dietrich entered into a partnership with the Thai owners of Krating Daeng and created the Red Bull brand that we know today, launching it into Austria in 1987.

This is a classic example of someone with a corporate career who took his marketing experience to develop an existing product into a new brand, creating a new category in Western markets, which today sells billions of cans worldwide!

There are loads of good examples of business heroes in the drinks category as it has always been receptive to new product ideas, but we think that Dietrich is probably top of our list.

In summary

Even if the motivation to start your own business is strong, you are still likely to feel challenged to make the move when you start to think about practical realities and the immediate effect on your life. There is likely to be some impact on your finances, which can have a knock on effect on the financial security of those that share your life.

You need to take a thorough approach to reviewing the risks which will involve looking for the solutions as well as identifying possible problems.

Three key activities can help convince you that it is the time:

1. Calmly assessing your positions of power and strength. These will help reaffirm why you can succeed in business.
2. Assess the risks in advance and plan to mitigate them. A financial fall back plan to cover short-term income in case the business fails.
3. Reassure yourself of what you could realistically hope from starting your business beyond just the financial.

Chapter 3

Looking for inspiration

If you have been working for a large company for several years you are probably unlikely to be an inventor with a new product idea. You will need therefore to find a business idea that you can succeed at and for which there is a market demand.

If you are lucky, you will know what you want to do. For those who have been dreaming of a new business for many years, it is really about finding the right time and the right impetus to do it. If this is the case, you can feel free to skip the rest of this chapter, which will look at the sources of inspiration for a new business.

Searching for a new business idea

If you feel that you are struggling for ideas or have a number of ideas but are unsure of which option is the best, try to take a systematic approach in your decision-making. Work methodically through the sections below. Write everything down and you will be surprised how the ideas start to flow.

There are three sources of inspiration for a business:

- your historical experiences
- the opportunities present in today's market
- what you stand to gain by going it alone.

We would suggest a three-step process to help unlock these sources:

Step 1 – look behind you

One of the key themes in this book is the value of your experience and indeed this can be a great source of inspiration in a number of ways.

1 Review your career to date

In your working life you will have collected lots of experiences, including:

- Job skills:

  Most people who work for large organisations have a job specialism. Whether you have worked for one company all of your life or have spent time in a number of companies, you are likely to have evolved some specific job skills.

If your job includes a professional skill, this would open up specific opportunities to sell that skill. This is the most obvious route for a new business idea. For those that have professional qualifications, such as accountancy, legal or medical, it is easy to see how selling these skills via a stand-alone business could have potential. Obviously, establishing the demand for such a venture is important but we will address this in Chapter 5.

Most people with a corporate background will have a functional skill, even if it is not of professional status. Functions such as marketing, sales, project management, HR and so on can lend themselves to a consultancy type business with these skills either positioned as an "expert" consultant back to the corporate world or more likely as a external source used by smaller companies who cannot afford or do not need full time employees to undertake the associated jobs.

Experience of managing people is a job skill worth noting as this could be important if you create a business where you expect to need employees.

- Job experiences – you may get some inspiration from the companies or type of businesses you have worked for:

  Have you enjoyed working in a particular industry or with a particular product or service sector?

  Have particular jobs or companies given you additional skills, e.g. becoming a trainer or mentor?

  Working in a particular sector can mean that you develop a particular expertise, e.g. the pharmaceutical industry, telecommunications, food and drink, etc. which to all intents and purposes is an additional skill.

  Can you identify through your past job experiences people who may be able to support you in the future either through their contacts or by giving you business?

Sometimes inspiration can come from seeing others doing a job badly.

Finally, before you move on from reviewing your job experiences, there is some benefit in couching this thinking with reflections on your strengths and weaknesses. This is a time when honesty is definitely the best policy and if there are any outstanding strengths or real weaknesses in your game it is ultimately in your interest to factor this in. Even if this does not add to your thinking on a new business idea it will eventually be useful when you consider what skills you need in the venture to make it successful.

2 Life experiences

Don't limit your thinking to your career. Also take the time to think about the things you do and have done in other areas of your life. Try to identify the things that:

- you are good at
- you enjoy
- you are skilled at
- you would like to do.

In some respects, this can be the most fruitful area for inspiration as it allows you to potentially merge your loves in life with your job:

Again, take a methodical approach and record your findings:

- *Skills.* You probably have a range of skills that are related to hobbies, sport, voluntary work and so forth that may be a source of a new business idea. Try and think about how these skills sit alongside your job-based skills. It is often the case that again as we get older we get increasingly more "expert" on our recreational activities.
- *Loves.* What do you really enjoy spending your time doing when you are not working? Think about how much easier it would be to get up in the morning if you were going to be doing something you love all day? Can you think of a way in which you can apply your business skills to a recreational product or service that you also know a lot about?

- *Strengths and weaknesses.* Again, it is worth taking the time to think through these potential opportunities in the context of your strengths and weaknesses. You may love cooking but are not competent enough to be a chef. If you love chocolate but are a diabetic, it might not be the best idea to open a chocolate shop!

Step 2 – look around you

It is often said that there is no such thing as a new idea. We are not sure whether we agree with that, and certainly don't want to get into a philosophical discussion on the topic. However, one thing is for sure, if you take the time to look around you there is a ready source of new business ideas to inspire you. Here are just a few things to think about.

1. Look for areas of growth in the economy for instant inspiration. Do not be put off because someone else has thought of the idea first. Look for businesses that are succeeding and explore if there is room for you.
2. There are several easy sources of market research available in the form of newspapers, trade journals, blogs, etc. As with all research, some caution should be applied especially if you believe you can bring something new to the market. If Henry Ford had asked people what they wanted from their transport in the early twentieth century, they would probably have said "faster horses"!
3. Can you see an opportunity to do something better? It may just be a British thing, but we seem to spend an inordinate amount of time complaining about the quality of things we buy or the service we get. Can you see an opportunity to provide a product or service better than the current offering on the market? We live in a world where people are prepared even in times of recession to pay for perceived added value whether they offer better quality, are ethically sourced or save time/resources.
4. Regional opportunities – the world is becoming a smaller place all the time and this opens opportunities for you to be able to source products from afar into a more local market:

- Can you provide a product or service that is currently available elsewhere in the country or the world into your local market?
- There is a very rich vein of consumer interest in locally sourced products. Could you use your business skills to bring local products to the market?
- Think about products, services or businesses that you have seen abroad.

5 Can you see a gap in the market? This is usually the most difficult area – finding opportunities for genuinely new products or services is very hard but clearly not impossible as such new ventures continue to emerge. More often a refinement of an existing concept can fill a gap, and the children's travel suitcases, the "Trunkies" missed by the experts on BBC's *Dragons Den* might be one good example.

6 The opportunity to team skills – sometimes you will improve your chances of succeeding with a new venture if you are not alone:

- Think about your friends and colleagues; you may find that there are opportunities to marry up your business and management skills with someone else's physical or creative skills.
- There are obvious and major advantages to having business partners, but also an equal number of dangers. Where you have purely complementary skills with your prospective partners, whilst this strengthens your businesss, it does mean there are more mouths to feed, which will impact upon your potential profitability. Equally, you need to be sure that you have compatible attitudes and working styles with your partners, otherwise your new business can get as bogged down as any normal corporate institution.

7 The virtual opportunity. There has never been a better time for virtual businesses – online shopping is huge and the fastest growing area of the retail trade. Can you see opportunities to meet the on-line consumers' need with a product with limited online provision or indeed where the on-line provision is of poor quality?

8 Franchise opportunities: franchising can provide a ready-made concept for your business venture and a ready source of ideas. The dynamics of a franchise operation are different in many ways especially in terms of the legal and financial model for your business. This has a number of advantages, not least that the concept and the basic way of running the business are all laid out for you. Moreover the franchisor company will provide support for you throughout, providing the product or service usually, the marketing tools and administrative support. On the other hand, they generally lay down quite strictly what you can and cannot do, and obviously also you have to pay to buy the franchise and ongoing royalties.

So in many ways, owning a franchise is only stepping half the way out of corporate life, in that certain aspects of being an employee will remain in place as you still have to abide by franchise rules. However, for many people this is an ideal situation; they still enjoy the extra freedom of working to their own convenience and the added motivation of feeling that they work for themselves.

The franchise industry runs numerous well-publicised shows around the country that will help you understand better what is involved and the widespread industry options that are available. It is worth doing your own research and due diligence by talking to existing franchisees before paying for any such licence. Some ideas and offers are less well established and you need to be sure that the franchise idea you are buying into can work in practice and is not set up merely to earn money by selling the franchise areas.

Even if you do not wish to go down the franchise route the trends can still be a source of ideas for small companies as they often indicate areas of potential for small businesses.

Franchise information sources

www.thebfa.org British Franchise Association
www.thefranchiseshow.co.uk
www.franchisedirect.co.uk
www.thefranchisemagazine.com
www.whichfranchise.com
www.theukfranchisedirectory.net
www.the-franchise-shop.com

9 Buying a business. If a franchise is not for you, there is still the option to buy an existing business and within certain sectors this remains the most common way of starting up. The retail sector for instance, whether it be a newsagent, dry cleaners, restaurant or pub, are types of operation typically purchased from an existing owner. These opportunities are advertised both locally through press and board advertising and through a number of national listing agencies. The agencies advertise regularly in the national press and also list online a wide range of all industry types and organisations that are for sale. Browsing through these can actually be quite thought provoking in its own right. The agencies can be briefed to help you find a particular type of business, or within a very specific area of interest or geographical location.

As with all such purchases, if you decide to pursue interest in buying a business it is vital that you perform enough due diligence to ensure that the business is exactly in the state it is purporting to be. This will inevitably involve some formal legal advice and possibly some accounting help too.

Businesses for sale contacts

www.business4sale.co.uk
www.business-sale.com
www.rightbiz.co.uk
www.businessesforsale.com
www.daltonbusiness.com
www.turnerbutler.co.uk

10 Niche opportunities. Do not be afraid to explore niche opportunities. Small can be beautiful. Today's consumers are very receptive to choice, which is conducive to developing specialised products:

- Think about large markets with limited choice of products.
- Think about sectors where one or two companies may dominate.
- Think of specialist needs dictated by religion, health, age or infirmity.

A good example of this is the recent development of the cider market. The sector had been dominated by a very small number of large companies selling one style of cider and was fairly static. As small businesses entered the sector positioning their products as better quality, the interest in the category was invigorated with new styles and flavours driving the growth.

Step 3 – look ahead

Finally, as part of this systematic approach to finding inspiration for your new venture, do not forget to look forward.

There are certain global and local trends in markets and demographics that you should consider when searching for your inspiration. You may for instance consider the increased life expectancy and growth in population of retirees to present a long-term opportunity for your business. On the other hand, you might believe that alternative energy provision will have an ever-increasing market that you can help fill. It clearly makes sense to go into a business that has future growth potential and so looking ahead to judge where markets and trends are likely to move will be a valuable exercise. And if nothing else, an important question to ask of any idea you may have. Will it have long term potential?

But possibly the greatest inspiration of all is to try to envisage how it will feel to have your own business.

You are your own boss, have your hand on the financial risk tiller and can steer your own destiny. Think about the rewards of running your own company both financially and emotionally and the benefits of being independent. More than anything, this should spur you on.

The power of experience

Hopefully, if you haven't already nailed your new business idea, this chapter will have been some help.

Your experience is unique to you so don't underestimate it.

You have a plethora of experience which can be utilised both from years of working for other people or from your personal out-of-work experiences.

- You have specific job skills, developed and honed over the years. If you have always worked in the marketing field but have no wish to have a business that focuses on selling those skills, you can still be confident that whatever your new business is you will be good at marketing it.
- You have commercial skills, which have often developed even if you haven't had a financial based job. Managing budgets of any type in a large company will have exposed you to many of the principles you will need to run a small business. Often the levels of budget responsibility in a large company will still be greater than those involved in running an independent venture.
- Broad-based business skills. A key benefit of working in a large successful operation is that we are exposed and absorb business skills from other parts of the company. So if, for example, you have always worked in sales you will have had a lot of interaction with marketing. If you are fortunate, you have probably gained exposure over time to a broad base of skills including HR, finance, marketing, sales, legal, all of which you may find helpful in your future venture.
- Your contacts – don't underestimate the value of your contacts. If you have spent time in corporate life then you will probably have a long list of past and current colleagues, friends, suppliers and customers that you have developed over the course of your career who could prove helpful in the future. Even if you do not immediately see how or why these contacts may prove useful in the future, take the time to establish a database of contacts and know how to reach them. The existence of on-line social media sites can help with this. www.linkedin.com
- Finally, perhaps the most important aspect of your experience is maturity. Maturity comes with age and experience and puts you in a different place to a younger/ less experienced individual. Your maturity will help you deal with the unpredictability of running a company. It will present itself in the form of confidence in your decisions, a grounded perspective on issues/problems and opportunities.

TIP Once you have the outline of an idea for your new venture try creating a mini CV for yourself outlining your qualifications for this role.

If we reflect back on our own start up at Ubevco, it was clearly the power of our experience that led us and our future trading partners to believe we could succeed with our particular business.

Firstly, our job skills complemented each other and we shared experiences in relevant product categories. We had all the key bases covered – sales, marketing, finance and logistics which was very helpful as we were positioning the business as a sales, marketing and distribution service to international drinks companies. As importantly, we shared some relevant experiences which were not job specific in four areas.

1 *Developing brands.* Dennis and Catherine had both worked for many years in sales and marketing roles in blue chip brand companies, essentially developing brands. But even Chris with his finance background had worked for the previous 10 years in companies that focused on selling brands, firstly in an advertising agency and then for Maison Caurette.

2 *Managing and importing other people's brands.* We also had a great deal of experience individually and collectively working on other people's international brands. Working on other people's brands is different from working for an organisation that owns the brand. Lines of authority are often longer and more complicated. Working on a brand from elsewhere in the world also carries the responsibility of (1) making the brand successful in the new market and (2) keeping the brand positioning in sync with the other international markets.

3 *Drinks experience.* The third area of shared experience was in the drinks industry. We had all worked for many years – probably over 30 years between us

– for different companies and across different drinks sectors including lager, ale, stout, wine, spirits and soft drinks.

4 Contacts. We had worked individually and collectively on a number of brands, which provided us with the source of our business. The personal relationships that we had with the brand owners were important in securing their business. Importantly, having these brands on board allowed us to hit the deck running on day one of our new business. There were also other contacts such as bankers, marketing companies and logistics contacts that had faith in us and agreed to work with us to get us on our way.

As individuals, we could all lay claim to significant experience but put this all together and the case for the three of us was very powerful:

- managing drinks brands
- managing agency brands
- experience of UK drinks sectors
- broad-based business skills.

Your personal expertise is very important at the time of your start up – as you need to also convince other parties that you will succeed.

We return time and again in this book to the subject of utilising your own experiences in your new business. It doesn't have to mean that like us you carry on in precisely the same industry, but your business strengths will have emerged from your experiences and it is vital you tap into these in your new life to help ensure your success.

In summary

New business ideas can come from many sources and it is important that you dedicate some time to developing your core idea. This is your opportunity to come up with the best business for YOU.

- You may already have had your core business idea in the back of your mind for years, just waiting for the freedom and opportunity to be released. Even so, you need to ensure that there is a sustainable position for your business in today's market. Take the opportunity to do your homework/market research to endorse whether it is a good enough business opportunity.
- If you have not yet finalised your business idea, you need to use your relevant experience to guide you to some options. Look at all your job and life experiences to establish what you are good at and what you enjoy doing.
- Once you have your idea, you can evaluate whether you progress by starting up a new business, buy a franchise operation or indeed buy into an existing trading company.
- Any finally, in weighing up your options, you need to consider the issue of going it alone or with other business partners, particularly if there are some colleagues in a similar situation following redundancy. The decision to go it alone or with partners is certainly a big one.

Chapter 4

Leaving employment

Irrespective of how clear and committed you may be to becoming your own boss, before you can do so there are some important things to think about regarding your immediate situation.

You will be facing one of two possible scenarios:

- leaving your job of your own accord
- being forced to leave your current employment.

Whichever situation applies to you, we firmly believe you need to proactively manage it. In redundancy situations it is possible to feel that you are just a pawn with no opportunity to influence the next move. However, there are always things that you can do to ensure the best possible outcome for you. Whatever the circumstances, you need to feel empowered that you are part of the management process.

Resigning from your employment

If you are currently employed, then clearly the decision to leave is yours. Feeling positive or negative about your employer may be influencing your decision to change your career direction but you need to ensure that your emotions do not affect your behaviour when you leave.

The effective management of your departure might be very important for your future success. It is hard to generalise, but it is very possible that your new business will have some connections with your employment:

- You may be planning to set up in competition to your employer.
- You may see an opportunity to be a supplier to your employer.
- You may be trying to purchase a part of the organisation.
- You may want to use contacts that you currently use as part of your job.

Even if you intend to move into a completely unrelated business, we would suggest that it is always better to be a "good leaver" not a bad one. If you and your employer end the relationship with good grace and in a professional manner, then you will be saying good things about each other long into the future. That will invariably help; the positive things you say about your past employer will work its way around the trade or industry you operate in, and of course vice versa. For that reason, we would suggest being as open and honest as possible with your employer about your reasons for leaving and future plans.

Before you begin any conversations with your employer, you need to consider both your employer's possible reaction and your contractual position. There are several scenarios to consider:

- If you are to become a competitor, they may react negatively to your resignation and plans. They may wish that you stop work immediately, placing you on "garden leave", which may or may not be desirable according to your specific situation.
- You may be working on projects that your employer really needs you to complete.
- You may be able to help your employer to recruit your replacement.
- You may be able to be flexible about your notice period.
- Timing may be relevant if there is a seasonal nature to either your current job or your new business.
- The tax year might also be a factor – utilising your tax-free allowances from employment for instance if income from your new business is likely to be slow or delayed.

In any event, it is sensible to consider all possible and likely scenarios in advance of telling your employer your decision. You can therefore be prepared for whatever their reaction might be.

Many employment contracts will have clauses in relation to your ability to compete with your employer after you leave, and whilst these usually relate to your joining a rival existing company they are likely to apply equally to your own business. Employment legislation does not look favourably on employers trying to restrict the right of individuals to earn a living and so it is unlikely to be a factor that stops you from making the change out of corporate life. You should nevertheless be confident you understand whether there are any effective restrictions that your contract might impose upon you.

Sources of help in this regard are noted at the end of this chapter, or you can take up specific legal advice by consulting a lawyer direct. Clarity is always best though and if it were a feasible option in your particular circumstances, written agreement from your employer as part of your overall resignation process would be ideal.

If there is no real sensitivity about your new business competing with your old employer, there might even be circumstances where you continue working, perhaps part time, whilst starting work on your own venture. Inevitably, you will have started the formulation of the idea during your personal free time whilst still employed, but it may be possible to combine physical employment in both for a period. We would not recommend doing this without permission, as this probably breaches your terms of employment and is certainly very questionable ethically. However, there may be a lot of merit in the right circumstances in this arrangement as it gives you some continued assured income whilst establishing your new business and allows a longer smoother handover for your previous employer.

If this kind of arrangement seems like a mutually sensible fit, this is something you should plan to suggest when you first discuss your change in career path with your employer.

There were several instances at Ubevco of senior employees sharing their plans with us.

In one situation, the initial discussions took place more than a year before the senior manager actually left. We were able to time his departure to best suit us both and he was able to work in his free time whilst still being employed on a lot of the pre-trading issues that he needed to complete. As he was starting up a business in an unrelated industry, there were no competition issues and so it worked perfectly for everyone.

In another instance, right back in the early days of our business, one of our employees wanted to start out on his own, actually within our industry. He shared his plans with us and we were able to find a way that he could develop his own business selling drinks but in such a way that it did not conflict with us. He ceased to be an employee, but still managed one specific area of business for us through his new operation. By openly discussing the situation, we ended up with a solution that helped us both.

By way of contrast, we had one employee who was fully employed as a salesman but unbeknown to the directors was also a licensee of a bar. There were some conflict of interest concerns with this, and these would have been manageable had they been raised and communicated ahead of time rather than after the event. At the very least, this situation seriously impacted upon the trust of the individual concerned.

So in dealing with the here and now of a continuing employment, we suggest that you:

- take the time to think about all the issues – for both you and your employer;
- decide upon the best solution for you;
- think about the ways in which you can sweeten the pill for your employer;
- share your plans if at all possible in an open and honest way – a good employer can usually help not hinder.

Dealing with redundancy

The economic pressures prevalent for much of the twenty-first century and the relentless march of technology have combined to make people in employment ever more expendable.

However, for a potential entrepreneur, being made redundant can provide the final push to take the plunge. Not only does it force one to make a decision about what to do next, a redundancy payment can also provide some financial support.

In a situation where your employer is looking to make redundancies, employment legislation requires a formal consultation process with the employees. This can be done individually or, if it involves 20 or more redundancies, collective consultation is formalised. Specific time periods are allotted for the process, which includes appointed representatives to look after the employee's interests which might involve trade unions in some circumstances or elected employee representatives.

In most cases, these consultations should present opportunities for voluntary redundancies. In a situation where you are already minded to leave the corporate world, this will present an ideal opportunity to leave with some financial compensation as well as the feel good factor of helping to preserve someone else's job.

A properly run redundancy will also set out the financial remuneration package that the employer is offering. There are statutory minimum amounts payable that are linked to number of years completed service and the age of the employee. In most cases, the employer will formulate their own scheme tailored to the service contracts they have in place. Redundancy payments in the UK (but not unpaid wages) can generally be paid tax free up to a maximum of £30,000 (at the time of writing). A well-managed redundancy will often provide independent legal advice to the employees, but this is also available through a number of free services.

The consultation process is mandatory and should your employer have failed to engage in this process then you may well have a strong claim for "unfair dismissal" which can award enhanced payments to the redundant employees. Once you become an employer yourself, you may well bemoan the level of protection now afforded to employees, but the redundancy legislation is in our view very fair and allows both parties to deal with a difficult situation in a professional and open way.

All employees should have contracts of employment and it is important to be mindful of any responsibilities that these set out for the employee. Especially relevant will be any clauses that relate to your ability to compete with your employer, hire former colleagues and deal with customers or suppliers of the company that you are leaving. In general, it is increasingly difficult for employers to try and enforce such restraint of trade clauses especially when the employees have been made redundant. However, we always favour clarity and seeking some advice (see Sources of free redundancy advice at the end of this chapter) and this is a sensible first step. If your plans are not likely to be controversial in the eyes of your employer, try and discuss the issues with them. Building into your termination agreements an amendment or cancellation of any of these contract terms should be possible and a wise measure.

Whilst impending redundancy may turn out to be the biggest break of your business life, the process is still usually stressful with often periods of uncertainty and apparent inaction from the employer or administrator. In addition you may be leaving friends and colleagues of long standing whose circumstances may also be uncertain and coping with the emotional stress less well than you. The consultation process is all designed to try and alleviate these issues and communal support is usually very beneficial.

Be conscious of your own internal and external "PR". There can still be negative connotations about someone who has been made redundant as to whether it was true redundancy or a mask for removing an underperforming employee. It is sensible therefore to be aware of this and ensure that any business contacts that are likely to be part of your future understand the real position. This might be as simple as ensuring that any key people know ahead of time that you are volunteering for a redundancy programme. When it happens it is a good news event without any thought that it was precipitated by your work performance.

Generally speaking, redundancy, which forms part of a corporate headcount reduction, will be well managed by the employer, who these days will be well versed in the proper and sympathetic procedure. On the other hand, if your redundancy follows the corporate failure of your employer and thus lies in the hands of an administrator or liquidator, our experience suggests that this is much less likely to be the case. Unlike an employer, the administrator has no personal relationship with the individuals concerned and the focus will be much more financially oriented.

With the demise of higher profile businesses such as high-street chains and football clubs in recent years, the acts of an administrator have begun to attract some media attention and public interest. Whilst one would acknowledge that their primary role is to work for the benefit of the creditors, there seems to be a recurring perception that they do not always effectively communicate with employees through the redundancy process. Given the level of fees that they seem to command, one would have thought that they could afford to manage that aspect just as well as any company organising their own redundancy programme.

Sources of free redundancy advice
www.acas.org.uk
Citizens Advice Bureau www.adviceguide.org.uk
www.direct.gov.uk

In summary

The first step to becoming your own boss is to leave your place of employment. By giving this consideration ahead of time, you may find you can gain some additional benefits.

- Try and be a 'good leaver' as it will smooth the process and have potential benefits for the future.
- If you are being made redundant, ensure that you play a proactive role in the process, as there is much for you to gain.
- Look for opportunities that may help you in the short term as you start up your new venture, which at the same time can offer advantages to your employer.
- Whether you have been made redundant through corporate downsizing or receivership, or whether you have been bold and resigned of your own accord from your employment, the end result is the same. You are now free of the responsibility of employment ready to move forward with your plans.

The way you are treated as an employee has a dramatic effect on how you perform in your job and also on your long-term loyalty to the business. In the future you may find yourself to be the employer. Take care that you factor into your actions the impact it may have on your colleagues and employees. If you remember how you wanted to be treated as an employee, you may engender better relationships with those you work with in the future. Taking care to protect the dignity of others costs very little but can earn you great co-operation.

PART 2

BUILDING YOUR BUSINESS PLAN

In this second section of the book, we are going to look at the key initiatives that you need to undertake in the start up period for a new business. Essentially, these are the things that you need to do before you get to the point where you can start trading.

1. Firstly, we will discuss the importance of developing your core idea into a meaningful proposition. This will in turn help you formulate reasonable goals and enable you to develop a strategy to achieve them. This is the important first stage of constructing your overall *business plan*.
2. You need to create a *financial plan* that allows you to manage the key elements impacting upon the potential success of the business, including a profit forecast, cash flow and balance sheet. We will offer guidance on their preparation and illustrate with simple examples.
3. How and when you use external advisors in the business will depend on the type of business you have. We will discuss how to determine the right time to use external advice so that you do not waste valuable resource paying for something you can do yourself.
4. You will need to decide how to structure your business, both in terms of who owns it and the legal entity you choose to operate under. We will look at your options in this chapter.
5. Deciding on a name is the first step in establishing your business brand. You will also need to develop a range of other tools including logo, stationery, websites and so forth which will begin to give your business its unique identity and be available to use as you launch the business.
6. All good business management involves an awareness of the risks that the business faces. It is especially important in the start up phase and many a young business has floundered because it neglected to assess and manage risks. We explore the key ways to minimise your exposure to such issues.
7. The encapsulation of all your planning into a final formal business plan creates a valuable tool that you can use with the people you need to influence to help make your business a success. It is the culmination of much of the thinking in the book thus far and signals that you are ready to start the doing!

Chapter 5

Developing the idea

In large companies the process of developing business goals and strategy usually takes place at elevated levels often by the PLC board and will likely involve external consultancy help. It may be therefore that you have not been directly involved in the process. It is probable, however, that with a corporate background you have been involved in business planning and strategy at some level and this experience will therefore stand you in good stead.

In this chapter we are going to talk about some basic business principles. We are not trying to teach you to suck eggs rather hoping to help you to consolidate your thinking.

We are going to look at three areas:

1. The core proposition of the business – this fleshes out your basic business idea into a clear competitive position.
2. Setting your business goals – this defines your long-term aims for the venture.
3. Developing your business strategy – identifies how you will achieve your goals.

Once you have these three things sorted, then everything else will fall into place easily. It is critical that these three areas form part of a joined up piece of thinking. You need to ensure that your goals are sensible in the context of the opportunity afforded by your business idea. Your business strategy will then identify how you can reach your goals.

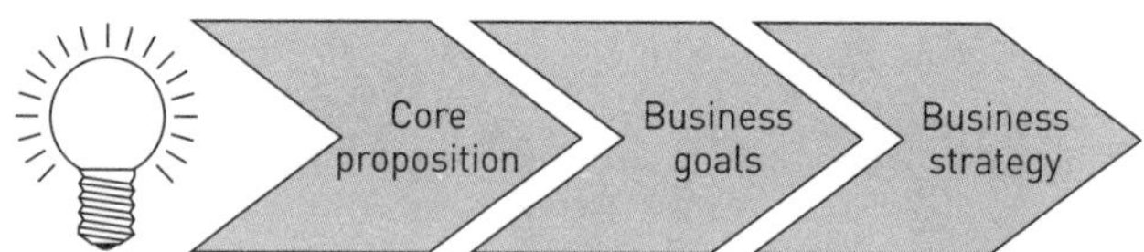

In the medium to long term you may choose to review and amend one or more elements of this planning. In the short term though, it will enable you to move forward in a logical and co-ordinated way as you structure the various aspects of your new business. It does not matter whether you are planning to have a business that just involves yourself or a large-scale venture; the process is equally valid and valuable.

The Core Proposition of the Business

Once you have developed your thinking as far as a final idea, you are well on your way. At this point there is lots to do before you get the business off the ground. You may need to secure finance and/or financial backing, you may have premises to find and negotiate, you may have to hire people, etc. All of these things will be important and you will be eager to get into the 'doing' stage.

Whilst it is important not to pontificate too much, it is also sensible to take the time to really clarify exactly what the core proposition of this venture will be. This does not need to take up too much time and if necessary can be done alongside other preparation, but it is imperative that you do not miss out this stage of your planning.

The core proposition develops your idea into a clear and focused statement that describes succinctly what your business is all about. This should include:

- the nature of your product or service
- what it offers that is different
- how it will deliver the difference.

We suggest that you think about this in as simple terms as you can. You should try and create a written statement that explains to anyone who might come across your business, what you do, why you do it and why it will be successful.

Our own example from Ubevco was brief and to the point:

Core proposition

- Ubevco is in the business of sales, marketing and distribution of premium packaged drinks.
- As sole representatives of international brands, we specialise in genuine imports.
- We focus on building brands.
- We are independent.

Your core proposition needs to clearly explain the concept of your business. You also need to think about all the elements of your idea, which combine to create a winning proposition. It is best to do this systematically by listing out all the relevant things that support the business idea. It is likely that this will include some that relate to the internal aspects of the business and others which relate to its position in the marketplace which it intends to work in.

And so, as a start point, you need to consider both the internal and external factors that are relevant.

Internal factors

The internal factors of support include all the things that are essentially within your control. This will include:

- Describing your product or service offering.
- The unique elements to it. This is possibly the most important element and if nothing else this acts as a challenge for you to determine why you will succeed.
- It should include how you intend to deliver this product or service into the market.
- Any trade-specific benefits.
- The consumer benefits.

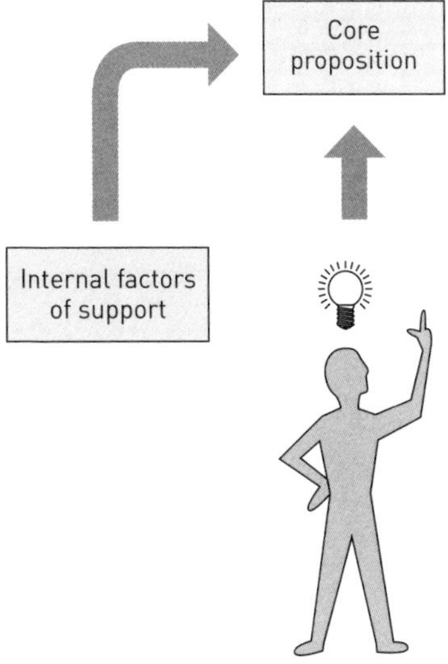

External factors

The external factors of support are the things that you may not have direct control of but that you need to either manage or at least be aware of as they form part of your product offering. For example:

- You may be creating a new sector within an existing marketplace.
- You may be taking products into a new location.
- You may be targeting a growth category.

All such factors add power to your concept.

This is also an opportunity to check that there are not any things out there that can cause you a problem.

- Is there room in the market for you?
- Can you quantify the size of the opportunity?
- Do you know your competitors?
- How are they likely to react when you enter the market?
- Is there growth in the market?
- Are there any specific government agencies or legal issues pertinent to your business?

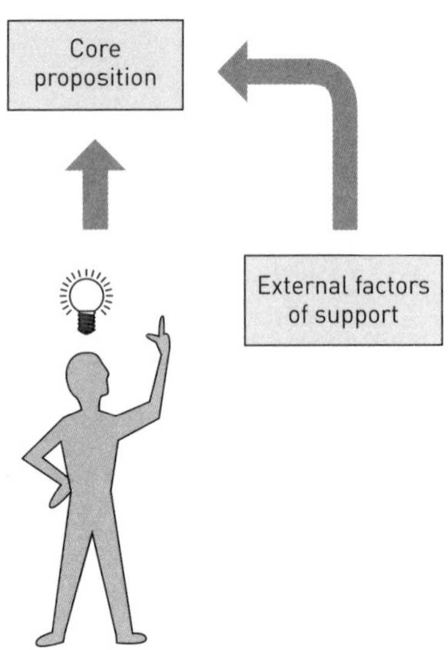

Quantifying the market opportunity may be difficult but if you do not attempt to do so, you will find it harder to set realistic business goals.

You may think in your own mind that you are clear on your core proposition already. Great, then you won't find any difficulty in putting it down on paper. The aim is to create a statement that really spells out why your business is unique, including both internal and external factors.

There are three benefits to doing this:

1. It will confirm to yourself that you have a focused business proposition.
2. You can use it early on before you have a fully worked business plan to explain to others what you are trying to achieve and why they should support you. For example:
   - bankers
   - suppliers
   - customers
   - employees
   - potential investors/partners.
3. You can continue to use it throughout your business life to check if you are on track and focusing on the right things.

4 Once you are satisfied that your business idea is clear in your own mind, then it is worthwhile sharing it with friends, family or colleagues. Ask for their honest feedback. Does the feedback match your understanding?

Core proposition
- Ubevco is in the business of sales, marketing and distribution of premium packaged drinks.
- As sole representatives of international brands, we specialise in genuine imports.
- We focus on building brands.
- We are independent.

Internal elements
- Focus on small range of premium brands.
- National sales team.
- Network of distributor partners.
- Sell through to end consumer.
- Long-term brand building.

External elements
- Large numbers of international brands want to export to UK.
- Distribution options limited for international brands – large brewers or wholesalers.
- Consumers want choice of genuine brands.

At Ubevco we saw an opportunity to fill a gap in the market. That was the inspiration behind our core idea. To create an agency business that could compete with all the large operators in the UK drinks market.

The options for international brands were limited at the time. There were three options:

- they either had to set up their own operation, which was financially prohibitive until they reached a certain scale;
- manage their brands through either the large UK brewers or wholesalers who usually had bigger priorities with their own brands; or
- use small agencies who had limited reach due to their size.

We saw the opportunity to sell our combined experience in the industry with a proposition, which gave brand owners what they wanted – a business with enough scale to reach the whole UK market and able to offer real focus on the brand.

The independent element of the proposition was key for two reasons. Firstly, being independent in the market would allow us to work with anyone and everyone, as we had no vested interest in any one brand. Secondly, it endorsed the importance of being our own bosses in charge of our own destiny.

Setting your business goals

When you are clear on your proposition then you are in a position to get into the real planning of your business. This should include three stages: setting business goals, developing your business strategy and finally a working plan.

Setting your business goals is not the same as setting your business targets. Your goals put a perspective on your aims for the next three to five years.

Even so, you should try to make them as specific as possible. Where relevant you can state your volume and/or share targets, your profit targets, service levels, etc. – any elements that you perceive as important to the success of your business. Remember, you are now the boss so you are aiming to deliver the business profit to you and your partners – not to some invisible board of directors higher up the organisation.

We set ourselves some very simple goals:

1 to become the UK's leading independent premium drinks agency; and
2 to earn reasonable profits.

These goals were consistent with our proposition. We were aiming to sit between the large operators and the small distributors. It was currently a vacant position. If we achieved the first objective of being the leading independent drinks agency, then we knew from the market data that we would have sufficient volume to create a healthy business.

Our company credentials presentation sets out these goals.

Ubevco Distributors Ltd Corporate Aims

– To become the UK's leading independent premium drinks agency business by:

- focusing on a small portfolio of strongly branded products on an agency basis
- focusing on selling the brands through to the consumer in all trade sectors by investing in an account and field sales salesforce
- establishing a national network of key distributor partners to develop the brands and not to be a direct supplier to the retail trade
- working closely with the distributor partners to sell through the brands to the end consumer by investing in a trade marketing resource
- taking a long-term approach to the market and investing in brands

– To earn reasonable profits.

Our profit goal may seem a bit obvious on the face of things. However, this statement served three purposes:

1 A profit objective is normal for corporate aim and indeed it is healthy to have one in a private company.

2 The statement of 'reasonable profits' was in the spirit of a balanced, fair and open relationship with our brand owners. It clearly implies that we did not intend to take too much profit and were prepared to invest back into the business.

3 The statement of 'reasonable profits' also implies that we are not prepared to make losses. This was equally important for our brand owners to understand.

Developing your business strategy

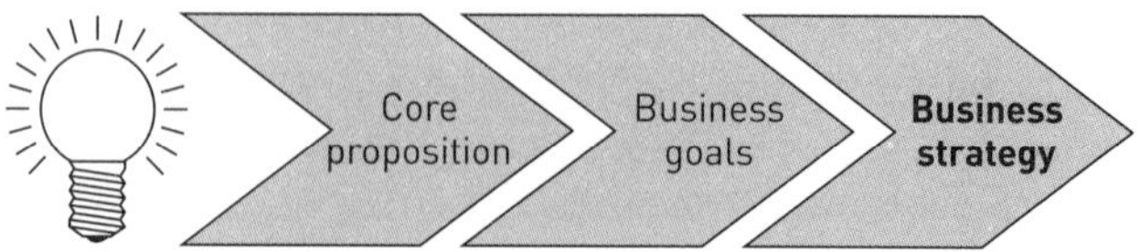

Strategy determines the clear direction we must travel in order to achieve our goals. It is how we set out the competitive position in order to achieve our objectives and identifies our distinctive offering or competitive advantage. If therefore we deviate from that strategy, it is likely that we will experience consequences in regard to the achievement of those goals. If part of your core proposition is to be price competitive, then plans that include price promotions are strategically consistent. If, however, you are positioning your business as a premium supplier, then cutting price is strategically inconsistent.

As with goals, strategy should be clear, focused and simple. It will be the reference point for the development of short term plans – to check if plans are consistent with our aims.

Importantly, *strategy* should not be confused with *tactics*. Strategy is always a planned function. Tactics are usually reactive to a particular situation or problem. Sometimes you have to take tactical decisions that are inconsistent with your strategy, but they should be done with caution. Tactically, you may decide to run price promotions but do not pretend that this is on strategy as it could serve to undermine a key part of your proposition.

Again, you can see from the statement in our company presentation, our strategy was simple. In order to achieve our goals we set out to do the following:

- exclusive supply in the UK;
- only work with a small number of brands;
- establish a network of trade partners to allow us to reach all areas of the UK;

- build brands with an emphasis on long-term growth versus short term.

We stayed true to this strategy – it was not complicated which meant everyone in the business understood it.

The simplicity of the strategy meant it offered clear guidance and it undoubtedly underpinned our success. We frequently came across opportunities for extra volume that were not on strategy, e.g. the chance to add more brands was tempting, as it would add income. However, this would have affected our focus and therefore undermined our competitive advantage.

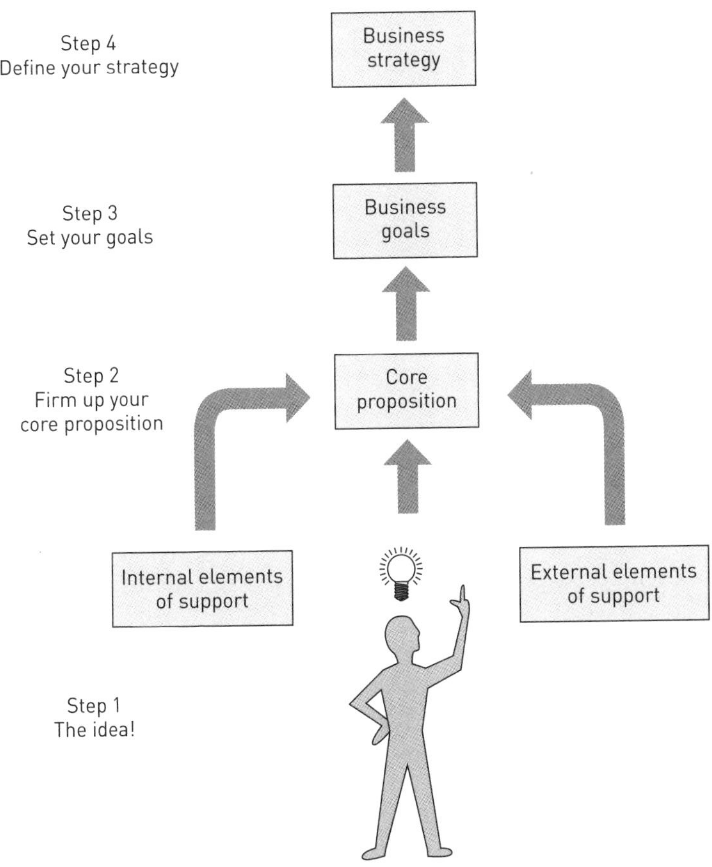

The time you take to go through the process of business planning will be very valuable to your long-term success. It need not take too long, but relative to its importance this will be time very well spent.

In summary

In this chapter we have set out how you should develop your business idea into a fully thought through core proposition which is an accurate summative of all the key elements of your business.

1. Think through the factors both internal and external that will contribute to it.
2. Set your business some medium to long-term business objectives, which will guide your success.
3. With your goals in mind, set out the strategy which will ensure that you can deliver your goals.

Once you have done this, you will be ready to create your working plan!

Chapter 6

Number crunching

With your proposition, goals and strategy all now clear in your mind; it is time to produce your *financial plan*. The aim of this plan is to enable you to assess your start up needs, provide confirmation that your venture can work as a business model and to act as a working tool for you to manage the business through the early days.

The financial plan will form the backbone of any formal overall *business plan* you produce for potential bankers, investors or other stakeholders in your business. In this chapter we will give some guidance on the production of what is effectively your budget, a key element of the final, formal business plan.

Preparing your financial plan

It can be very common for some business owners to regard the financial plan as just bean counting and equally common for those businesses to fail. Whilst you may be most excited about your new business idea, your financial plan is the very essence of your business; it's what you are in business for. Without knowing and planning exactly how you are going to generate income, manage your costs and pay your bills, you will not be able to earn your living and continue to operate.

One of the reasons some owners glaze over when the talk turns to numbers and budgets is that they think it is too technically demanding, but like most things in business life, it really isn't and certainly doesn't have to be. In your life as an employee you will probably have been involved in some parts of a budget process and have some skills in that regard. In reality the principles of business budgeting are no different, nor particularly more complicated, than managing your home finances.

Whilst your proposition, goals and strategy thinking will all relate to the medium, even long term, the working plan will be much more focused on the short term. Typically, you need:

1. a detailed month by month budget for the first year; and
2. a broader plan for the second and third year, maybe on a quarterly basis.

Spreadsheets were pretty much designed with this application in mind. They enable you to amend and update your model through time very easily. If you have no spreadsheet skills then seek some help in setting one up. It is important that the input of the core assumptions must be yours.

TIP If you do not know how to use a spreadsheet, now is a good time to learn. It is not difficult and will stand you in good stead for the future.

We firmly believe that as with all things, the simpler and more focused the budget the better. The key is to identify the main income and expense drivers of your business and set out what you can reasonably expect these to deliver. These drivers are inevitably linked and interdependent, but we will focus first on income generation.

1 Sales budget

Start building a budget income model from the base up. By this we mean you do not just set out a sales revenue number for each month, rather analyse how this is built up. By way of example, imagine that you are starting a business that is to supply water coolers to offices. It is likely that your sales may fall into three parts:

- providing the initial cooler
- selling refill bottles
- annual hygiene cleans.

You would then set out, by month, the further relevant parameters such as:

- how many offices you believe you add as customers each month
- how often existing customers will re-order refill bottles
- how many bottles per order
- sales prices of each of the three types of sale.

Finally, you may build in some "seasonality", which in the case of bottled water might be that in the summer people will tend to drink more than average compared to winter months. A simple spreadsheet (see below) can then be constructed which quickly and easily builds up your sales forecast for your first year.

New Water Cooler Limited

Year 1 Income Plan

	Jan	Feb	Mar	Apr	May	Jun	Jul	Aug	Sep	Oct	Nov	Dec	Total
Distribution & Rate of Sale													
-New Customers	10	10	10	10	10	10	10	10	10	10	10	10	120
-Total Customers	10	20	30	40	50	60	70	80	90	100	110	120	120
-Refill Frequency per month	1	1	1	1	1.5	1.5	2	2	1.5	1	1	1	1
-Bottles per order	2	2	2	2	2	2	2	2	2	2	2	2	2
Sales Prices													
-Cooler Installation	£200	£200	£200	£200	£200	£200	£200	£200	£200	£200	£200	£200	£200
-Refill Bottles	£6	£6	£6	£6	£6	£6	£6	£6	£6	£6	£6	£6	£6
-Annual Clean (6 months)	£25	£25	£25	£25	£25	£25	£25	£25	£25	£25	£25	£25	£25
Sales Value													
-Cooler Installation	£2,000	£2,000	£2,000	£2,000	£2,000	£2,000	£2,000	£2,000	£2,000	£2,000	£2,000	£2,000	£24,000
-Refill Bottles	£120	£240	£360	£480	£900	£1,080	£1,680	£1,920	£1,620	£1,200	£1,320	£1,440	£12,360
-Annual Clean	£0	£0	£0	£0	£0	£0	£250	£250	£250	£250	£250	£250	£1,500
	£2,120	**£2,240**	**£2,360**	**£2,480**	**£2,900**	**£3,080**	**£3,930**	**£4,170**	**£3,870**	**£3,450**	**£3,570**	**£3,690**	**£37,860**

We appreciate, of course, that not all businesses lend themselves to this kind of income build up model, and so for example if you are a consultant aiming to work on single projects at a time, then your model will be much simpler. However in our experience such an approach does work for most business types. In our own consultancy practice we are amazed by how many new venture owners are preparing their plan based on sales figures that are essentially just plucked from the sky. When the owner is encouraged to break down these figures into numbers of orders, visits, customers, etc. it will usually produce a very different and more realistic picture.

If this sounds complicated – it's not. It is little more than a proper sense check on deliverability but it is extremely common for it not to have been properly thought through. Watch any programme from the TV series *Dragons Den*, and you will see how, as soon as they have heard the new idea, the dragons begin to ask questions about how the sales are built up, sense checking the numbers. It is at this stage that so many of the would-be entrepreneurs get thrown out of the den as their sales projections are exposed as having no realism.

In this way, you now demonstrate real substance as to how your sales are going to be produced and by using this build up method; you will become comfortable that your budget is realistic.

2 Cost budget

It will also help you to properly set out the costs associated with producing those sales. In this case, for instance, the delivery costs will be linked to the number of orders your model has identified.

Having produced the sales budget, you need to go through the same process to access your costs. With the detailed analysis of the sales projections many of the costs will flow naturally; the cost of those sales (the cost of your product to you), any delivery or other variable costs that are directly related to the orders you take. In addition to your variable costs you will also need to assess any fixed costs (i.e those which do not relate to how much you sell) including things such as your salaries, premises, marketing and administrative costs.

New Water Cooler Limited

Year 1 Cost and Profit Projection

		Jan	Feb	Mar	Apr	May	Jun	Jul	Aug	Sep	Oct	Nov	Dec	Total
Sales		**£2,120**	**£2,240**	**£2,360**	**£2,480**	**£2,900**	**£3,080**	**£3,930**	**£4,170**	**£3,870**	**£3,450**	**£3,570**	**£3,690**	**£37,860**
Variable Costs	**Unit Cost**													
Water Cooler	£35	£350	£350	£350	£350	£350	£350	£350	£350	£350	£350	£350	£350	£4,200
Water Bottles	£2	£40	£80	£120	£160	£300	£360	£560	£640	£540	£400	£440	£480	£4,120
Cleaning material A	£4	£0	£0	£0	£0	£0	£0	£40	£40	£40	£40	£40	£40	£240
Cleaning material B	£2	£0	£0	£0	£0	£0	£0	£20	£20	£20	£20	£20	£20	£120
Transport Cost	£5	£50	£100	£150	£200	£375	£450	£700	£800	£675	£500	£550	£600	£5,150
Total Variable cost		**£440**	**£530**	**£620**	**£710**	**£1,025**	**£1,160**	**£1,670**	**£1,850**	**£1,625**	**£1,310**	**£1,400**	**£1,490**	**£13,830**
Fixed Cost														
Office & Warehouse		£200	£200	£200	£200	£200	£200	£200	£200	£200	£200	£200	£200	£2,400
Staff Costs		£1,250	£1,250	£1,250	£1,250	£1,250	£1,250	£1,250	£1,250	£1,250	£1,250	£1,250	£1,250	£15,000
Admin & Marketing Costs		£300	£300	£300	£300	£300	£300	£300	£300	£300	£300	£300	£300	£3,600
Total Fixed Cost		**£1,750**	**£1,750**	**£1,750**	**£1,750**	**£1,750**	**£1,750**	**£1,750**	**£1,750**	**£1,750**	**£1,750**	**£1,750**	**£1,750**	**£21,000**
Total Costs		£2,190	£2,280	£2,370	£2,460	£2,775	£2,910	£3,420	£3,600	£3,375	£3,060	£3,150	£3,240	£34,830
Profit/(Loss) By Month		**-£70**	**-£40**	**-£10**	**£20**	**£125**	**£170**	**£510**	**£570**	**£495**	**£390**	**£420**	**£450**	**£3,030**

Once you have added this analysis to your sales analysis, you will have a clearer view of the financial viability of your business.

You will have a financial budget that is showing your operating profit, which is essentially the profit the business will produce before any interest or taxation. The information that has enabled you to produce these figures will be the key data to drive the second part of the financial budget.

3 Pricing

These simple models use invented sales prices and costs that seem to work, but clearly arriving at the price for the goods or services you are going to sell to your customer is a key issue. A successful financial plan is really down to some very simple principles:

1. Are you selling your goods/services at the right price?
2. Are you buying in your goods/service at the right price?
3. Are the "bits" that you do in between the buying and selling being done cost effectively?

There is no magic formula we can provide to help you set your pricing as every market operates in its own way. What you must do is research your own particular market, and get comfortable that you are capable of managing these three elements competitively. There may well be complexity even within markets and pricing might need to change according to the location and type of customer, or the level of work you need to perform to affect the sale.

This is a constant issue for your business, and something that should be under permanent review. As circumstances change, so might your costs or sales prices and your ability to react and adapt will be a key part of being a successful management.

4 Paying yourself

The simple answer to the question of what you should pay yourself is "What the business can afford". However, for planning purposes you should build in a salary for yourself. We would suggest you budget for this at the lower end of the salary range you would have to be paying if you were hiring someone externally to perform this role. In this way, your financial plan is giving a realistic view of the true business performance rather than one masked by the fact that you are not drawing the proper wage for the job you are doing. That is not to say you should necessarily pay yourself that salary if the business begins to underperform, and the cash flow restraints might also mean that you draw a lower salary for a while until you get back on budget. Thankfully, the converse is also true, and one of the great attractions of it being your own business is that when it starts producing extra profit – you can have it! Some element of caution is recommended though, and it is wise to retain some of any additional profits in the business to help bolster its financial position as well as your personal one. It means you are building a war chest within the business to help you through any leaner times or unusual occurrences in the future.

By way of illustration, when we started ubevco we set our salaries at around half the rate we had been earning in our previous employment (even though these had barely been at market rate). At this level we had sufficient income to meet our personal obligations and it worked within the financial plan to help demonstrate a profitable business. Each year as we hit and beat our targets, we were able to pay ourselves a bonus or dividend and gently increase salaries back to full market rate. We also though established a rule from the start that a given percentage of each year's profit would be retained in the business to help build reserves. The strength this gave the limited company financially helped with negotiating terms with bankers and suppliers as well as ensuring we could see through the leaner times which came later.

5 Cash flow forecast

The cash flow statement literally plots each month how much cash you have in the business. All the budget forecasts above aim to show you how you perform over the course of a year, especially your profitability. The cash flow statement will show you if you have enough cash in your bank account to pay your suppliers, staff, tax, and so on whilst you wait for your customers to pay you. Without cash in the business you will quickly fail unless you have taken steps to manage it.

At this point, things do get a little more technical and getting some help from someone experienced in producing balance sheets and cash flow budgets might be beneficial if you feel it's beyond your skills. Again, it is important that you make the decisions on the key assumptions that will drive the model, as you will be the one managing and ensuring these assumptions are met or improved upon.

The key assumptions that you will need to build your cash flow forecast are:

- how quickly your customers will pay;
- how quickly you have to pay for your goods;
- payment terms for other suppliers (e.g. rent, telephones, vehicles etc.);
- PAYE and VAT payments if appropriate (these dates are fixed for you);
- how much stock you will have to carry;
- initial investment and set up costs (any equipment, vehicles, website, marketing).

These factors will enable you to produce a sensible cash flow forecast and balance sheet.

The cash flow forecast will enable you to assess the funding requirement of your business which will in turn produce for you an interest cost figure. In the simple New Water Cooler example, sufficient initial investment has been made to ensure that no borrowings are required and so there is no interest cost. However, where there is interest, this will be added to your budget to finalise your pre-tax profit, which in turn will involve making allowance for the taxation you will have to pay in due course on this profit.

We should point out that the cash flow forecast and balance sheet will tend to show your overall financial position at the end of each month. You need also to be wary about your cash flow forecast between each month end. To that end, it is sensible to produce a short-term weekly cash flow forecast too, even if this is just for the first three months to check that you do not have different requirements or cash flow pressure that arise in mid month.

So your financial plan emerges, month by month year 1, and maybe quarterly for years 2 and 3. This is your budget. In arriving at the final version, the beauties of spreadsheets are that you

New Water Cooler Limited

Year 1 Monthly Cash Flow Forecast

		Jan	Feb	Mar	Apr	May	Jun	Jul	Aug	Sep	Oct	Nov	Dec
Cash Flow													
Receipts													
Initial Investment		£3,000	£0	£0	£0	£0	£0	£0	£0	£0	£0	£0	£0
From Customer Debtors	30 days credit	£0	£2,120	£2,240	£2,360	£2,480	£2,900	£3,080	£3,930	£4,170	£3,870	£3,450	£3,570
Total Cash In		**£3,000**	**£2,120**	**£2,240**	**£2,360**	**£2,480**	**£2,900**	**£3,080**	**£3,930**	**£4,170**	**£3,870**	**£3,450**	**£3,570**
Payments													
Water Cooler	60 days	£0	£0	£350	£350	£350	£350	£350	£350	£350	£350	£350	£350
Water Bottles	30 days	£0	£40	£80	£120	£160	£300	£360	£560	£640	£540	£400	£440
Cleaning material A	30 days	£0	£0	£0	£0	£0	£0	£0	£40	£40	£40	£40	£40
Cleaning material B	30 days	£0	£0	£0	£0	£0	£0	£0	£20	£20	£20	£20	£20
Transport Cost	monthly	£50	£100	£150	£200	£375	£450	£700	£800	£675	£500	£550	£600
Office & Warehouse	30 days	£0	£200	£200	£200	£200	£200	£200	£200	£200	£200	£200	£200
Staff Costs	monthly	£1,250	£1,250	£1,250	£1,250	£1,250	£1,250	£1,250	£1,250	£1,250	£1,250	£1,250	£1,250
Admin & Marketing Costs	30 days	£0	£300	£300	£300	£300	£300	£300	£300	£300	£300	£300	£300
Total Cash Out		**£1,300**	**£1,890**	**£2,330**	**£2,420**	**£2,635**	**£2,850**	**£3,160**	**£3,520**	**£3,475**	**£3,200**	**£3,110**	**£3,200**
Net Cash Flow		£1,700	£230	-£90	-£60	-£155	£50	-£80	£410	£695	£670	£340	£370
Cumulative Cash Flow		**£1,700**	**£1,930**	**£1,840**	**£1,780**	**£1,625**	**£1,675**	**£1,595**	**£2,005**	**£2,700**	**£3,370**	**£3,710**	**£4,080**

can play with various scenarios and see what impact a change in assumptions can make. This may then lead to you considering whether an additional employee might enable you to increase the customers by using your model as a working tool to assess the impact of adding such resource.

It is very common to produce a pessimistic version and an optimistic version to review alongside the main budget. Banks will often ask to see what happens when you run such sensitivities and it helps to already be on top of that question when they raise it. So having some of these sensitised versions prepared is good practice, but you should still have a firm budget that you are committed to as your plan.

TIPS

- The budget is the budget; do not be tempted to change it.
- This allows you to compare performance to a base set of business assumptions.
- Cash flow forecasting is vitally important, so get help to produce this if you need it.

6 Working tool

Whilst your budget should be cast in stone as your original budget, the spreadsheet itself can be continuously manipulated to change assumptions, rates of sale progress or changes in costs and prices as time progresses. It is common to report your business each month showing actual results against budget, but also to produce a rolling forecast to demonstrate how results to date and any change in the assumptions you originally planned now impact on what you believe the business will produce. This is your working tool.

The fact that you have built the sales model up will allow you to understand, explain and tweak these assumptions on a continuing basis and form an essential working tool for you to manage your business. Inevitably, not everything you built into the plan will work out exactly as you assumed, and applying changes to the model will help you assess ahead of time the impact of these alterations. They may for instance have an impact on your cash flow and any adverse change can be managed through continual monitoring of your financial plan.

Ubevco						
DAILY SALES REPORT	14th January					
Period	January					
Day	8	of	20		40%	
	SALES TODAY	Sales period to date	Target period to date	Target total period	% Target achieved	Period projection
Packaged						
Castle	180	2,204	2,548	6,369	34.6%	5,510
Cermoc other	30	57	0	0	-	143
Dos Equis	16	564	572	1,430	39.4%	1,410
Gambrinus	60	98	0	0	-	245
PU packaged	566	2,487	3,208	8,020	31.0%	6,218
Sol	2,745	10,777	10,492	26,229	41.1%	26,943
Tiger	2,873	26,197	27,297	68,243	38.4%	65,493
Total volume	**6,470**	**42,384**	**44,117**	**110,291**	**38.4%**	**105,962**

As you start to trade your income forecast model will help you focus on whether you are on track. You should regularly monitor progress. In Ubevco we did this daily at a top line level. Each night the sales for the day were issued to the entire staff showing a projection for the month compared to budget. It was simple – everyone, everyday knew how we were doing.

In summary

The production of your financial plan and first year budget brings some reality to the core proposition and strategy. It can sometimes lead to some re-addressing of your thoughts and plans if they prove to be commercially unviable, but more often it is more a tweaking process and will enable you to construct a workable target.

The financial plan ideally should cover the first three years in overview with month by month detail for the first year. It should include:

- sales budget
- cost budget
- which generates therefore a profit and loss budget
- cash flow forecast
- balance sheet.

This element of the planning process will form part of the finalised business plan but will also become the working tool that you need to measure and amend your progress as the business kicks into life.

Chapter 7

Getting advice

As you move through the process of firming up your core proposition and start developing your business plan, you may have started to question whether you need advice. We discuss here in more detail when and how you might need some external help.

Trusting your experience and instincts

If you have chosen your business correctly, you should not need external advice about your core activity – you are the expert! You have already created your proposition, formulated a strategy and confirmed there are good prospects in the market for your operation.

That is not to say that you might decide to outsource some aspects of your operation, but we make a clear distinction here between out-sourcing and advisers. Outsourcing can be a very useful tool for most businesses, where a particular function can be managed more efficiently that way – usually due to the economic advantages of specialisation. With outsourcing you are specifying and managing the service, whereas we see an adviser as someone who is potentially influencing you in the way you manage your business. We will return to the subject of outsourcing in detail in Chapter 12.

We believe that businesses and their owners/management seek external advice for four distinct reasons:

1. *Knowledge gap.* Obviously, if an entrepreneur does not have detailed understanding about a specific aspect of running their business; they need to supplement their knowledge through an external expert. The easiest example would be tax or legal advice, which require detailed professional expertise but not on a continuing basis. Almost every company needs to utilise such advisers, and for a start up business this is often needed before inception.
2. *Reassurance.* Managers or owners in a business often seek re-assurance regarding their business decisions and this is often a prime motivation for seeking advice.
3. *Save time.* Sometimes you might need advisers purely and simply to deal with a matter that you do not have the time to handle.

4 *Indecision.* The fourth category might represent one of those frustrations that may have driven you from corporate life. This is the situation where advice is sought to either support or even prompt a management decision. This can be motivated by company politics, lack of confidence or most often to protect the decision maker's backside. If the external consultant has recommended a course of action, then the management feels protected.

At Ubevco, the brands we exclusively represented in the UK came from major international brewers with large corporate structures. The European marketing director of one such brewer needed to consider whether and how to promote one of his brand's that we handled in the UK. Rather than use his own expertise to make what was a relatively small financial decision, he hired a marketing agency to make a recommendation to him. This agency duly produced a report, largely based on extensive interviews and fact finding with both our company and the brewer themselves. The real experts in the subject were the European marketing director and Ubevco management – not the marketing agency. It is an all too common trend within larger corporations to abrogate responsibility for decisions by hiring consultants.

The person in our example didn't lack expertise or ability; rather he wasn't encouraged to trust his instincts and experience, largely because of the corporate culture. This led to his feeling that he needed to justify his decision – cover his back. We are sure that should he give up the day job and start his own business then he would not countenance paying for outside advice in these circumstances.

The value of external advisers

Let us consider the situations where a new or young company should consider bringing in external expert advice.

Reasons to refer to an external adviser

To fill a KNOWLEDGE GAP	To seek REASSURANCE	To SAVE TIME	To overcome INDECISION
Financial reporting	Sounding board	Recruitment	Strategy analysis
Taxation	Extend business network	Cost reviews	Business planning
Employment legislation	Experience sharing	Trade Intelligence	Opportunity assessment
Health and safety	Second opinion		
Insurance	Emotional back up		
Other corporate governance			
Should I use one if I am a fledgling entrepreneur?			
Yes, to fill your gaps	Maybe, if it's free!	Try and avoid	No, you are the decisive expert

As a new business owner, your appreciation of your cash resources and your profit and loss account will act as a natural deterrent from hiring external advisers. This is a good thing, but you will need some support particularly from your "knowledge gap" advisers.

Your knowledge gap advisers

- The most obvious example of these is an external accountant. Almost every business needs an accountant, whether it is to perform audits if you are a limited company, to produce accounts for banks or to advise and assist with your taxation affairs. Moreover, you need to consider the best formal structure for your business before you start trading. We will discuss this issue in greater depth in the next chapter, but your accountant is often best placed to help you with making this decision.

You will certainly need an external accountant once your business is up and running, and this is likely to be a long standing relationship that will help you through the financial and taxation aspects of your business life.

- To a lesser extent, the same can be said about retaining a lawyer for your business. At some stage you will come across some situations where you will need legal services. Increasing bureaucracy means that there are a whole raft of issues that the business owner now needs to ensure he is compliant with, particularly in areas of employment laws and protections as well as the ever-popular health and safety legislations. However, in recent years specialist support companies have been developed to cater for the SME market offering online and telephone support services to handle such regulatory issues for relatively modest annual fees.

  www.lawontheweb.co.uk

  www.lawsociety.org.uk

- A third and often overlooked adviser is your insurance broker. A long-term relationship with an adviser can be very beneficial to your business. A good business insurance broker can provide invaluable advice to ensure that you take steps to minimise the risks in your business. He will also have products and ideas as your business changes and grows that can be very helpful and financially beneficial.

- Other useful sources for advice:

  Government site offering general advice on business start up: http://www.businesslink.gov.uk

  HM Revenue and Customs advice: http://www.hmrc.gov.uk/startingup/

Seeking reassurance

What about the more nebulous areas we identified where we suggest a business might benefit from "reassurance"? As a small business, it is likely that you are the sole decision-maker and this can be a very lonely position where you have only a limited opportunity to explore issues with other people. There are some options to give you some external support.

- This used to be best exemplified by the "non-executive director" role whereby a company would appoint such esteemed figures to help advise and support the working directors. Certainly, this role is evolving, especially in quoted companies where the legal responsibilities of the non-executive directors have been highlighted and the role is much more focused on proper corporate governance.
- For a new SME, the role is now more frequently and better identified as that of business mentor, which usually comes without any of the legal responsibility of a formal board directorship. Many successful start-ups have related that they have benefited from having a mentor and this is something that merits consideration.

Do I need a business mentor or non-executive director?

Do you lack business strength or experience in a specific aspect?

Do you have a trusted business confidant?

Would you benefit from expanding your business network?

Do you have access to a second opinion or someone to act as a soundboard?

Do you need emotional support?

The answers for most start-ups will be yes, but these needs can often be fulfilled by:

- business partners
- colleagues
- family and friends
- trade contacts.

If not, you may need to make a more specific search for a business mentor.

These can be best sourced through people you know and it is helpful to have someone with whom you have some personal empathy; who understands you and your style of management.

Failing that, there are a number of business support bodies that help source business mentors for new businesses.

http://www.associationofbusinessmentors.org/

http://www.startups.co.uk/support-and-mentoring

http://www.growingbusiness.co.uk/

If you are convinced that a mentor or non-executive director will help your business, then you probably also need to consider whether they should have a financial interest in your venture, and we will consider that further in Chapter 8 as part of the wider subject of your business and ownership structure.

Time savers

Having suggested you will need your "knowledge gap" advisers and that you may benefit from "reassurance", we now come to those we have categorised as "time savers". These might include the recruitment consultant or a cost reduction expert, who will doubtless argue that their expertise, contact or supply base means they can more efficiently execute these tasks and are better placed to advise you on the best solution. In reality their main benefit is they are saving you time, especially in recruitment where the selection process can be very time consuming with application assessments and interviews.

As a new SME owner/manager though, you probably cannot afford to use this type of adviser and in our experience they will often not produce as good a solution as you would find yourself. They do not understand your style and culture as well as you do and this is vital in any employment process in smaller businesses. There is no room for people who do not "fit in" and the costs of bad recruitment are significant in lost salary, redundancy expenses and the repeated time and money involved in re-recruiting.

In Chapter 15, we will explore in more depth the process of recruitment, being as it is the important first step in the successful management of your relationship with your employees.

Indecision

Whilst we suggest you should try not to use the "time savers", we firmly recommend that you avoid using advisers in the "indecision" category. To seek reassurance is fine, but to hand over responsibility for formulation of core plans and strategy to an external adviser suggests you should be staying within the corporate world. To do so would be to betray your conviction that you are going to trust your own instincts and experience.

A young, entrepreneurial business should use advisers predominantly to bridge the knowledge gap and to seek reassurance, but rarely to use the time savers or indecisions. Mature, large companies are the reverse, they will have filled the knowledge gap with in-house lawyers, HR and tax specialists but persist in using outside consultants to steer them on core strategy. This is in part the result of complex decision making within larger organisations, their politics and the inability of individuals to make decisions and act quickly. These are probably many of the frustrations that led you to want to leave and become your own boss in the first place.

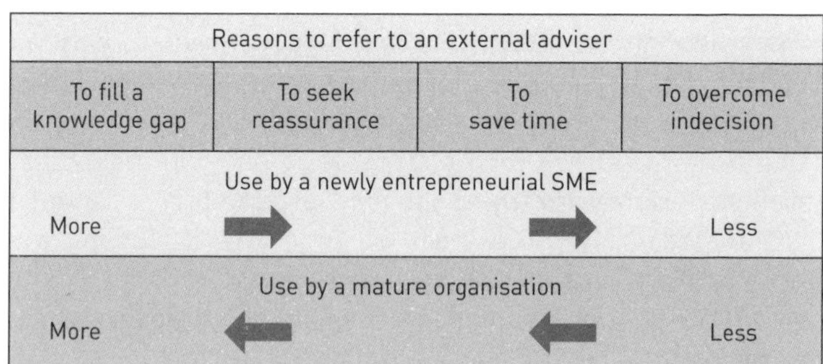

Reasons to refer to an external adviser			
To fill a knowledge gap	To seek reassurance	To save time	To overcome indecision
Use by a newly entrepreneurial SME			
More	→	→	Less
Use by a mature organisation			
More	←	←	Less

Non-executive directors

"When we started Ubevco, we had a non-executive chairman whose strength lay in his ability to raise external investment

from the City. We had worked with him in our previous company and we got on well. During our first year of trading it became apparent that our chairman believed we needed an injection of outside capital and had set up a potential deal to reverse into a shell company, a dormant property company listed on a minor stock market in the City. He believed that this injection of capital and enhanced status would help attract strong brands to represent.

As executive management, we believed that we already had an excellent portfolio of brands strong enough to deliver as much growth as we could manage. Moreover, our chairman's deal would have diluted us to just under 50% of the ownership, and we had no desire to return to a position where we did not have control of the business we worked in. We therefore agreed to disagree, and parted on good terms. We then had to decide whether we wanted or needed to replace him as non-executive chairman.

As a business, we were performing well from all perspectives, but we were publicity shy and the world at large did not appreciate what progress we had made since our formation. We had chatted after a golf day with an old friend from our advertising background, Tony Vickers who was Sales and Marketing Director for Sky TV but was soon to be semi-retiring. It soon became apparent that he would make an ideal non-executive chairman, not for his knowledge of our industry per se, but rather for his broader business acumen, contacts and status. He gladly bought his predecessor's shares and was appointed the new non-executive chairman.

The effect was almost immediate – the fact that Sky's Sales & Marketing Director was joining Ubevco made everyone take us more seriously and enhanced their respect for the company. Within two weeks he had been invited to Durban to speak to 1,000 delegates at a South African Breweries conference, and our staff and business partners were all impressed we could attract such a heavyweight chairman."

In summary

It is very easy for the would be entrepreneur to misjudge when they need external advice and getting it wrong can cost you valuable time, money and even talk you out of your best ideas. Our experiences suggest the following:

- Most businesses need help with specialist areas such as tax, formal accounting and legal matters.
- Choose empathetic specialists, most have the ability but they will be long term partners so you need to "get on".
- It is often valuable to have a second opinion for reassurance, this can come from colleagues, friends, business associates or a formal mentor.
- You are the expert in your business, so don't pass core decisions to external advisers.
- It's your business and the fulfilment comes from making the hard calls yourself.

Chapter **8**

The right business structure

The process of defining your core proposition and preparing a financial plan that convinces you that your business is feasible is essentially the same irrespective of how you plan to structure your business. Before you can start trading though, you will obviously need to decide the best legal entity in which to undertake your business, how the ownership of the operation is to be organised and who you want involved in that ownership.

Ownership

We will consider first who is going to own your business. Whether you are proceeding with the idea on your own, or with partners; in either case, you might also consider whether you want, or need; to invite others to become part owners.

We discussed in Chapter 7 the merits of having a business mentor or non-executive director and suggested how you might assess if you need one. We also looked at whether the same support and reassurance might instead be available from business partners, colleagues or family and friends.

If you have decided to seek this type of support, then the question will most likely arise as to whether you need to remunerate them in some way, possibly by offering them a share in the business. There are also other people you might wish to consider as potential shareholders, sometimes for just personal reasons but particularly if you need to raise initial start-up finance and cannot fund all of this yourself. There are six distinct potential owner groups to consider:

- spouse
- family and friends
- a business mentor (or non-executive director)
- other workers in the business
- a co-operative
- pure investors.

Involving any of these in your owner structure can potentially help share any burden of raising any initial finance that you need, and this has obvious attractions. But as with most things in life and business, there are pros and cons associated with any of the above potential shareholders.

Including your spouse or other family members as a co-owner is probably most frequently done, and is often largely driven by tax considerations. It may well be a tax efficient way to spread your income or business gains, the easiest example being to utilise your spouse's tax-free allowance each year by employing them in the business. Always remember though that if you are paying your spouse a salary, then they need to provide some services to the business to satisfy the taxman that it is a bona fide transaction.

Other tax efficiencies from spreading the ownership within your family might accrue later in your enterprise's life, for example, as it pays dividends or upon a final sale of the business. These though are situations that depend on individual circumstances, and it would be wise to further research your own position or take professional tax advice before making a decision. It is also important to point out that rules and regulations change with each Chancellor's budget and it might be unwise to make a long-term decision solely on the basis of what the current tax position and legislation dictates. Over the last decade or so, there have been significant changes in particular with regard to capital gains tax and also related initiatives to help encourage investment in entrepreneurial ventures. It would appear likely that this is an area of taxation policy that will be subject to further regular change as the economic climate remains volatile.

However, including the family in your ownership structure need not just be a tax driven idea. They may also provide significant moral and emotional support to you and the business, help you through occasional problems and provide extra help when it is needed. A cheap source of help is always welcome in any new venture. You may also have longer term ambitions to develop into a traditional family business, where several family members are employed and the business passes on through the generations.

On the other hand, involving the family can potentially cause problems and in particular things can get very messy when relationships change. It might feel very satisfying to include your children in the business ownership, but should they later get involved in, for example, an acrimonious divorce and their erstwhile partner seeks their share of the family business, it will be a complication that you can do without. Problems can equally occur between blood relatives over traditional business issues such as whether everyone is pulling their weight or performing adequately. This can cause family frictions that spill over and damage normal family relationships.

There is no easy answer; each entrepreneur will have to consider the pros and cons for themselves by thinking through all the possible scenarios, based on their own knowledge of the personalities involved.

In many ways, these same principles and concerns apply to any proposed business mentor and to the idea of sharing ownership with key employees. Where a business mentor is also an investor, then of course it is a core part of the deal that he will have a share of the business, and equally sometimes your mentor may be providing their advice and reputation in return only for some participation in the ownership.

Generally though, we believe that it is preferable to enjoin either mentors or key employees in profit or performance related schemes, by which we mean they earn rewards linked directly to the success of the business in the same way that a share owner earns dividends or takes a profit share. This is easily achieved through bonuses and tax legislation also now actively encourages profit related pay with attractive tax rates. In Chapter 15 we will illustrate how we utilised these principles within Ubevco.

The reason we suggest this is that, as with many of our suggestions throughout the book, simple works best! Having just a few owners significantly reduces the risk of differences of opinion and gives you less personal interest issues to deal with. It makes key decision making quicker and easier, but does not preclude you from the ability to court advice or second opinions from your mentor or your key colleagues.

One of your motivations for running your own venture is the ability to be in control, and this can be seriously compromised by not having a very simple share ownership structure that ensures you, and, if appropriate, your business partners have this control.

That is not to say that you cannot have a larger number of owners if you feel the circumstances merit it. But you must ensure you consider all potential issues that could occur and enter into a formalised agreement between all the owners that provides for a clear and acceptable solution to these kinds of problems.

At this other end of the scale, the numbers of co-operative businesses are growing through these times of recession. A co-operative business is by definition owned and run by and for the benefit of its members, whether they are customers, employees or residents. This perhaps may be most applicable in the context of this book, when a company, or part of a company fails and the employees and potentially the customer base seek to save the enterprise by establishing a co-operative for their mutual benefit. Whilst famous co-operatives such as John Lewis are large-scale businesses, still 40% of the UK co-operatives operate at a scale of under £100,000 turnover. If you are facing redundancy along with a number of colleagues through the failure of your employer, this may well be an option worthy of further consideration. www.uk/coop/

Choosing your business entity

Now that you have established how many owners are to be involved in your operation, you should be in a position to formally proceed to form your business entity. There are essentially three main options available for you:

1. limited company
2. partnership
3. sole trader.

Clearly, the option of sole trader is only available as an option if you remain happy to proceed on your own, and there are benefits to setting up this way. These include the taxation benefits, administrative requirements, running costs and ease of selling or passing on your business when that time comes.

Setting up as a sole trader is the simplest way of structuring a business. It will require you to keep proper records of your business income and expenses which you will report under the self-assessment scheme to the tax authorities annually. It is a very appropriate way to structure yourself if you are a "sole trader", but although it does not preclude you from hiring and paying staff, such a structure is unlikely to be beneficial for businesses that plan on growing in this way. Whilst it is efficient tax wise and there are very few additional running costs, being a sole trader will make life difficult in trying to raise any business finance and will also deter potential buyers when eventually you want to consider an exit from your business. Moreover, it offers no protection from personal liability for the business debts – you and the business are as one.

Partnerships are a very common way for two or more business owners to establish a structure for their business, although they also offer no protection from personal liability for business debts. Many professional occupations are organised as partnerships, for example general practitioner doctors were typically organised this way. Other professional bodies, such as lawyers and accountants, have rules that insist that they are set up as partnerships so that they can be seen to be personally liable for their business actions. This was regarded as a mark of their professional integrity and competence, but also enabled the businesses concerned to retain privacy regarding their financial performance. A partnership obviously needs to keep proper business records and report their results for taxation purposes, but they do not have to disclose results publically, which is perceived as a big advantage versus limited company status for these types of organisation.

Partnerships should be governed by an agreement between the partners as to how the business will be operated which will include how profits are divided and how partners can join or leave the firm. They can therefore be a very effective way of organising your business so as to allow partners to retire when the time is right, and for other partners to be promoted from employee or join from outside. The bigger accounting and legal firms are always in a state of transition regarding the ownership as partners join and leave, and this works very efficiently. There are a number of statutory provisions which set out a basic set of rules for partnerships in the absence of a formal agreement, but it is advisable to produce your own even if it is just a very simple set of understandings, and we will discuss these further shortly.

Registering a business partnership is quite simple, it merely involves filling in a few forms with the Inland Revenue and you are good to go. There are no other public reporting requirements and virtually no formal regulation, so the ongoing costs of maintaining the partnership are as little as your own expertise allows.

Being constituted as a limited company, is by far the most common and appropriate structure for those businesses whose aspiration is to employ more than a couple of people. In a limited company the business is itself the entity and is in theory distinct from the shareholders and management of the company. Hence, the term "limited", of course, as the liability of the business is indeed limited to the finances of the company itself. This was always perceived as the primary benefit of setting up your business this way. However over time, the law has increasingly sought to make directors personally liable for certain actions they undertake on behalf of the business. These are especially relevant where a company trades in situations where they might not be able to pay their debts and Directors are vulnerable to being personally responsible for the monies.

This negates some of the advantage of being constituted as a company rather than as a sole trader or partnership, where there is no such ambiguity and the owners and the business are as one, and thus the individuals are responsible for all business debts personally.

Nevertheless, the format of a limited company is still the most appropriate one for most businesses other than sole traders. Potential external investors and bank financiers will normally be expecting you to be constituted as a limited company. The requirement to publically and regularly provide information and financial results to Companies House means that it is much easier to establish credit lines and a business persona. Your customers and suppliers will also tend to perceive you as more substantial if you are a limited company, even if this is arguably an unfair conclusion versus a well run partnership. Being a company also facilitates any changes in shareholding and potentially a very clean sale of the business when the time comes.

Maintaining a company is more costly in that you need to prepare formal accounts and these may involve being audited independently. In recent years the audit rules have been relaxed to allow smaller companies to be exempt from audit, although you will probably still need professional help to produce the accounts for submission. Nevertheless, there remains strong regulatory control over companies which is enshrined in company law, although, in practice, they are perfectly easy to manage with a modest support from your accountants.

The original setting up of a company is cheaper and easier than it used to be, and now can be done online direct with Companies House at very little cost and without specific expertise.

In recent years, the concept of a limited liability partnership has been introduced which is essentially a hybrid of a limited company and a partnership. It limits the liability of the partners in the same sort of way as a company does, but also requires some public accountability and disclosure. The taxation is levied like a normal partnership, which has advantages, along with the ability for partners to join and leave the business too. The concept is quite new and so judgement is still out as to how attractive they are and what problems they may cause.

As far as the relative merits of taxation rates between companies, partnerships and sole traders, there is not really a simple answer. Although a company pays corporation tax on its profits generally at a lower rate than income tax is levied on sole traders and partners, by the time the profits are extracted as dividends then these differences reduce and the relative merits depend on individuals' own circumstances and the tax bands they fall under. It is unlikely that any budget will make one entity significantly more attractive than any other, as the tax authorities would want to seek to achieve as level a playing field in this regard as possible.

Finally, it should be noted that you are free over time to change from one entity type to another. It is not uncommon for a business to start life as a sole trader, then as the venture progresses move to be a partnership before eventually changing to be a limited company.

Shareholder/partnership agreements

These types of agreement should be in place for all businesses that involve more than one owner. They are the "pre-nuptials" of the business world and it is very important that you put one in place.

Agreements do not need to be complicated; they are there to set out how the business is to be managed and what to do when circumstances change. A typical agreement should cover the following:

- the purpose and nature of the business
- set out how management decisions are to be taken
- how often directors/partners should meet
- how additional management/directors can be appointed
- how profits/dividends are to be divided
- how salaries are set
- how communications are to be made
- how terminations can be exercised
- what expenses can be claimed
- how confidentiality is preserved
- how shares can be transferred/sold
- what happens on death or infirmity.

In reality, it provides a default set of rules that need to be followed, usually only when a disagreement or conflict arises. They are usually never taken out of the filing cabinet – and they are most often needed when the owners never bothered to have one done in the first place!

There are many free or low cost examples available on line, so there is no excuse for not putting this in place if you have fellow shareholders or partners. For example:

www.lawdepot.co.uk
www.contractstore.com

Tax considerations

We have touched upon tax issues a couple of times during this chapter, and it merits some further emphasis and comment.

It is very hard to generalise about the best way to optimise your tax position. This varies so widely according to individuals' own particular circumstances and also the business owners' attitude and ethics. We do though have some very clear views on how you should manage your affairs and relationship with the taxman. As an importer of alcoholic drinks at Ubevco, we had to pay the duty on all the drinks as we imported them, as well as paying VAT on sales, PAYE on all our salaries and bonuses and corporation tax on the company's profits. We estimated that in the 10 years of running our business, our payments would have totalled in the region of £100m – and yet we never even received a thank you card! It was particularly vital to us as an importer to ensure that we dealt with all taxation matters efficiently, promptly and simply.

You will always be able to find people who will encourage you to look at various schemes, often involving offshore operations, to lower your corporate or personal tax rates, particularly if you grow your business successfully. Whilst it is argued that many of these schemes are legal tax avoidance as opposed to evasion, our stance was that doing things simply gave you certainty as to your position for the long term. By paying all your tax without complication or creative schemes, you know where you are with little prospect of being chased or investigated over years for money you may already have spent.

The same applied to claiming business expenses. As owners we agreed we would never have company credit cards, nor did we chance having any borderline company "benefits". We had private medical insurance and company phones and that was about it, we did not even have company cars for most of our time at the company. Whilst we were ultra cautious, we felt very comfortable that it gave us piece of mind and moreover set a good example to our employees regarding claiming of expenses. The Inland Revenue will inspect any company as a matter of course, and we were given an exemption from reporting many expenses once they had seen the tight control and attitude we had to such matters.

So our advice regarding dealing with tax matters is consistent with most of our other recommendations – keep it simple!

In summary

Structuring your business needs some careful thought, but the appropriate solution can very often be straightforward and obvious.

1. Assess and be clear about who will be involved in the ownership.
2. Determine whether you are best served being a sole trader, company or partnership. If it is unclear then take professional advice.
3. Put in place a shareholders or partnership agreement.
4. Register your enterprise and you are ready to go.

Chapter 9

Branding your business

Branding is a means of identifying a business, product or service as distinct from others. If you are selling products and services to consumers, it is likely that you will have to think about how you will market them as part of your business model. But at this stage we are thinking more fundamentally about how to brand and market the business itself.

The amount of resource that you need to invest will very much depend on the sort of business you have. It is an area where there are a myriad of agencies that can help you but whether this is good use of your money is a question you must ask.

There are two simple stages to work through:

1. You need to create your (business) brand.
2. You need to create a plan to launch your brand.

Creating the business brand

Your venture will stand more chance of succeeding if it has a distinct image that your customers recognise and come to associate with excellence in whatever field of business you are in. There are a number of elements that can contribute to building your business brand:

- your name
- your logo
- your core imagery.

The aim is to have each of the elements giving strong messages about your business; who you are, what you do and why you are different/better/cheaper, etc.

Costa Coffee is a good example of effective business branding. Its distinctive name, logo and imagery all convey quality and a clear promise of what the brand will deliver to the customer.

Choosing a name

Self evidently your business will need a name. Sometimes the choice is fairly obvious given the nature of what you are doing. You may choose to use your surname, or even full name, if you are in professional services; essentially you are selling you!

There are specialist consultants to help you find "the best" names, but reverting to good old common sense will usually do the job. Certain businesses used to rely heavily on telephone directories and often used to try and start their name with the letter "A", and so you would call AA Taxis or similar, but in the internet age the skills required to attract the customer's attention are much broader.

A name that reinforces what you do, or who you are, clearly makes sense in many business fields. Other considerations are names that are memorable, easy to say or write, unusual or just sound nice. Short will normally be better than long. Google is a great example of an unusual name becoming an iconic brand. There is sometimes a tendency to be humorous, but a quick glance at any stock market list would suggest that they rarely become world famous, so it's usually best to play it straight.

The best names do not necessarily have to reflect the type of business you are in. The Virgin brand consistently ranks amongst the most trusted and recognisable in the UK, yet it initially had no obvious association with a specific industry. Other businesses though do benefit from saying it like it is; although even then not everyone will assume you do what you say you do.

An associate of ours bought a take away pizza operation in Brighton and decided on the name "Dial A Pizza" as it was simple and to the point. He was somewhat taken aback some months later when his bank phoned him to ask what his business did. So much for a descriptive name!

> *'Ubevco', we admit is a strange name*
>
> Originally, it was developed for another venture of Dennis's – the United Beverage Corporation – set up to import American soft drinks. However, we knew it was less appropriate for this new business.

> Dennis and I had to go away for a few days and promised to come back with a better name for the business. So we did much brainstorming and returned home with some interesting options only to find that Chris had needed to finalise a decision on the name in order to undertake some practical things like setting up contracts with customers.
>
> So, in fact, we used the Ubevco name because it was expedient. The business was already registered and it had a bank account set up.
>
> In truth, in some ways it wasn't a good name.
>
> - People pronounced it wrong.
> - People couldn't spell it.
> - We were always being asked what it meant.
>
> But, at the end of the day, it was memorable. In many respects, its quirky nature was in keeping with the personality of the business and it probably helped us stand out.
>
> Catherine

There is an argument that it matters less what the actual name is as much as what you do with it. Longer term it has to be memorable.

Logos

Once you have determined the name of the business you must decide how to visually display it into a business logo. The visual identity of your business is all part of the process of getting noticed, making your potential customers aware of you and creating a favourable impression. Even the simplest of businesses use logos, so think seriously about it. You will have to live with your logo for a long time. Once you have established it, it is difficult to change.

TIPS

- Any friends or colleagues with artistic skill can be recruited to help.
- The student population is full of would-be designers who might be happy to help for the price of a few cold beers.

Designing your corporate logo can be fun, and there is no shortage of specialist firms, both local and national that would be delighted to do it for you. Equally, this is the kind of task that you can get help with at little or no cost.

You will be using it on all your company paperwork so as part of your design process consider how it will look on something as small as a business card and something as large as the side of a van if that is appropriate for your business. Your logo needs to work on both.

Creating something that is relatively simple is usually best. Think about the colours you use, avoiding fashionable colours if possible.

There are so many design options readily available on the standard computer it is possible to create a simple logo yourself. If you recruit the help of someone else or an agency, just make sure that you retain the design rights and that you have it in a form that is then easy for you to use throughout your business without incurring cost.

Other forms of communication

Business stationery

Just about every business needs business stationery: letterheads, invoices, e-signoffs and business cards, to name a few. Additionally, you may need to create leaflets, brochures and catalogues. In today's world you can produce most of this at a very low cost.

You may be able to meet all your needs by creating it yourself on your computer. You can set up templates for most of your stationery including your business logo. Take care to keep the presentation looking professional. Avoid the use of multiple typefaces to create impact. It can look really messy. Rather use one typeface but vary the size and colour for interest.

If you do not feel you can do this yourself, then there are some very cost effective options available on the internet.

www.vistaprint.co.uk
www.beanprint.com
www.betterprint.co.uk

As your business grows and cash becomes more available, you can choose to upgrade and evolve your company logo and stationery but in the early days be prudent about how much you spend.

Website

All new businesses need to have a website. Even if you do not intend to drive any custom through it, your website will act as a basic form of communication about your company. It is often the first port of call for companies and consumers alike if they are considering using your operation. If you do not have a website, it will raise concerns about your validity as a business.

You should make sure that the site gives a clear message about who you are, why you can deliver excellent product or service, your goals and any unique selling points that you believe you have.

The extent to which you are intending to use the internet to drive your business will determine the type of internet site you need. If you need a sophisticated website to advertise your product and take orders, you may need to get some expert advice on the best way to do this.

The first step is to buy your url and thereby secure your website name, and this is easily done on line, for instance see:

www.nominet.org
www.names.co.uk

You can spend as much or as little as you want on designing your site. Free compiler and display services are available in many places but these nearly always come with third party advertising, which tends to make them look cheap and unprofessional.

A better option is to look for independent design services that have perhaps prepared sites that you have seen and like the look and feel of. Finding a local business can allow you to meet the designers and work more closely than a web-based business.

Normally for around £1,000 you can get a very professional

looking site, properly hosted and with access to your own email address that incorporates your business name. The key is to brief the designer well with the content and style that you wish to convey and they will probably produce several options for you to choose from.

This was how we produced our own consultancy business website through a small independent company called Ratart.

www.blackburngarden.com

which we believe is also a good example of the kind of basic information a site should include:

- what the business is
- who you are
- why your customers should use you
- how your business works
- where you can be contacted.

Alternatively, there are many low cost options available on the internet for a low monthly fee. These are suitable if you just need a simple website:

www.vistaprint.co.uk
www.1and1.co.uk

There are three elements of costs associated with websites: creating the website, acquiring your domain name and hosting the site. You need to be careful when you look at the costs to be sure what are included.

TIPS

- Keep the content clear and simple.
- Avoid having too much activity on any page.
- Keep the design style consistent with your logo and other business communication tools.
- Take care to make sure you check the cost of making changes to your website as you may need to do this in the medium term.

Launching your business

Once you have dealt with the design and production of all the elements relating to your company's communications, you need to think about how to create awareness of your new venture and ultimately create some business.

Putting together plans for launching your venture should be given real effort, as it is the means by which you will get your income moving quickly. In simple terms, you need to let your prospective customers know that you are open for business. Clearly, the nature of your operation will determine the options available to you.

Trade events

Trade events can be expensive to take part in but may be worth considering. Local business networks can be very effective both to get your new business known but also for useful local contacts.

Contacts

Having people you know spread the word about your new business can be very productive. Personal recommendations are very powerful.

Social media

The use of social media in the business context has taken off rapidly in recent years. Its relevance to your business will again depend on what you do and how you take your product or service to the customer. Inevitably, some areas of social media will be important. Industry-specific groups have developed on services such as LinkedIn, whereas media such as Facebook and Twitter can be important in helping spread the word on new ideas or products. These are fast moving marketing vehicles and you need to keep abreast of their developments and the opportunities they offer to help market your product or service.

Search engines

If your business wishes to directly source its customers via the internet, then the importance of search engines and understanding how best to extract value from the fees you will pay cannot be understated. A nice name and logo helps, but it's really all about getting to the top of the appropriate search queues, and that requires some skill and dexterity in making the engines recognise you ahead of others – oh, and money, to buy your way to nearer the top.

Local reputation

It's not all about the World Wide Web though, and if your business is to operate on a more local and/or traditional basis, there is still a place for enhancing your brand identity by being seen around and word of mouth.Things to consider are:

- sponsoring local events
- attending local shows
- local newspapers are always looking for content
- leafleting in the local area
- sampling in the local area.

Other PR

There are also now several entrepreneurial focused magazines and the national press have sections in the supplements focused on business start-ups. These can be helpful in getting you some brand recognition, though we sense that the coverage tends to focus on the young and very innovative type of entrepreneur. Many of these owners tend then to focus on their own profile rather than that of the business, and start popping up all over the place in the media on self promotion. Very often this is to the detriment of running the operation – far better to crow about your success at the end of your business career rather than when it's still establishing itself and not yet proven.

Other networking

Social media dominates thinking in the modern world with regard to networking, but the more traditional ways still have a role to play in marketing you and your business. Explore as many ways as you can of putting yourself in touch with your target consumer base, whether directly or through networking via other contacts, friends or business acquaintances.

This might be through school and college alumni, business or trade clubs and associations or just people who know people.

Marketing your business

Marketing is a long-term task. It would be very dangerous to assume that once you have launched your business the job is done. You have already completed a lot of the marketing thinking you need to do; you have thought about creating a product/service that has a market demand, determined the right place and worked out whom you are going to sell it to. At this stage, therefore, the marketing task is about ensuring that all your potential customers/consumers are aware of your offering on an on-going basis.

Most marketing activity carries a cost with it and justifying this expenditure is often a difficult decision. Sadly, it is not a science and there is not a simple way of calculating the right expenditure ratio to maximise return. Again, experience counts for a lot in this area of the business. Use your knowledge of the market, look at what competitors do and begin with a cautious plan as you will undoubtedly learn more as time goes by.

At Ubevco we were in the business of selling brands and so we focused most of our marketing investment directly in the brands, rather than marketing the Ubevco business itself. Driving brand volume had the greatest impact on the business profitability so this made financial sense. As the business developed we were able to build a team of brand managers who had two key areas of responsibility:

- developing marketing plans for both consumer and trade activity; and
- managing the expenditure in line with the agreed budgets.

All the marketing budgets were agreed annually in line with projected volume and margin targets and so were always affordable in the context of the overall profitability of the business.

Each brand would take a different marketing approach depending on the target consumer for the particular brand. Sol, for example, had a younger consumer profile and the marketing plans reflected this with a lot of activity aimed at music venues including sponsorship of clubnights. Castle Lager, on the other hand, focused much of its activity around sports events as Castle sponsored the South African cricket and rugby teams for many years.

Given the nature of the drinks market, it was also important to put trade promotion activity in place to ensure that the brands were developing good distribution.

In addition to the specific brand activity, as a business we also did a small amount of customer hospitality and attended the key trade events.

Most of the tools that you will use we have discussed already in the section on launching the business. Take the time to review what worked well during this time.

Of course, depending on the amount of activity that you determine you need, there are many hundreds of marketing agencies available to help you. If you determine that you need some specialised help to create marketing plans you need to find the right agency. There are so many marketing agencies around this can be a difficult decision. Recommendation from people or businesses that you know or contacts from your corporate job may provide you with options. Remember, though, that large companies are less constrained when paying agency fees and they are likely to use large and expensive agencies who have the capacity to meet their more complex needs.

TIPS

- Ensure that you set yourself meaningful targets for any marketing activity so that you can measure its effectiveness, e.g. increased sales, additional customers or more repeat purchase.
- Do not be afraid to use marketing activity that has been used before. Being innovative can be an important way of achieving standout from your competition but it is most important that the activity is effective. So if something works, do not be afraid of doing it again.
- Ensure that you are very clear on how the agency will charge you. There are often complex ways of remunerating marketing agencies. You need to understand how much you will pay for the work in total. Do not get caught out with hidden "incidental" charges such as postage, printing, etc. which can add up significantly.
- Finally, make sure that any work you commission is owned by you at the end of the project. This allows you to change agencies if you need to for any reason or indeed you can continue to use the campaign but manage it yourself.

Often, a good way to source agencies is to look at advertising or promotion campaigns that you think are good and/or appropriate for your type of business.

Again, a good source of creative help can often be found locally to you. Either in the form of a small agency or indeed at local colleges and universities where students are looking for relevant experience.

In summary

Branding your business is your opportunity to create a distinct identity that can endorse the core proposition of the business.

The important elements are:

- distinctive
- used consistently
- reflects the important things about your business.

It is easy to spend money to help you achieve this but this is usually unnecessary.

Aim to create a simple and professional logo that can be used on all forms of communication that you will use. Of primary importance in the modern world is to have a website presence, even if you will not actively trade through one. Other branding initiatives will vary according to your particular market, so draw up a simple plan to ensure your business gets known to its key customers.

Chapter 10

Minimising risk

In Part 1, we talked about your personal risk assessment in the context of changing your employment status. We now need to address risk from the point of view of your business.

Any business, new or old, is always subject to risks, many of which lie outside your direct control. The risks in a new business are higher; you have to establish and prove your plans in the marketplace and have little in the way of a financial cushion. Minimising the risk on your business is important for two reasons: it will promote the long-term success of your venture and it will protect the investment you have already made in both time and money in starting the company.

Your aim is to ensure that the impact of any risks on you and your business is such that it is unlikely to end in financial failure.

Adequate insurance

It is easy to overlook the need for insurance when you start up a small business. We have already placed a lot of emphasis on keeping costs down. But as in our private life, there are certain types of insurance that we should always have in place to keep our business safe. Even if you are working from home, you cannot rely on your normal home policy to cover any of your business needs as in nearly all cases the homeowner policies exclude business related activity and assets.

Business insurance does not have to be expensive, but it is quite specialised and the use of a broker is more helpful than when you are looking for personal cover. You will need to cover the usual types of things such as:

- premises
- contents
- vehicles
- equipment for replacement in the event of loss, fire, theft and the like.

Where your broker can particularly help is advising on the extent to which your insurance can then reimburse you if you are not able to trade normally. Such business interruption insurance certainly merits serious consideration, as it can help you preserve your business income after a problem. Cost is obviously an important factor, but many business policy premiums are in any event turnover related, and so the cost moves proportionately with your ability to afford it.

You will need to ensure that you have any legally required policies such as proper public liability insurance. There may be some types of insurance that are relevant to your particular type of business, e.g. cash handling or goods in transit insurance.

If you have employees, we would highly recommend that you consider some basic life and disability coverage. In group schemes the cost is low per head and in the event of the death of an employee pays out a lump sum (typically three or four times salary) which the company can pass onto the employee's family. Perhaps even more vitally, the permanent health insurance ensures that in the event of an employee being unable to work through illness or disability for a sustained period or permanently, the insurance pays a proportion (often around two-thirds) of their salary until normal retirement age.

The peace of mind this provides to the employer and employee is very valuable and ensures that you never run into any kind of moral dilemma should one of your employees have the misfortune to be unable to work.

And, when a rookie salesman, working his first week, in his brand new car, parks too close to the Thames at low tide, returns from a sales call to find it half submerged, it does not have to damage your premium. Fortunately, the rookie turned out to be one of our best salesmen so we forgave him eventually!

> When we started Ubevco with around 10 employees, we straight away decided to take out life and disability insurance. It helped to demonstrate a caring and professional attitude, which in turn gave our prospective employees added confidence that working for Ubevco might be a positive step.
>
> We could not afford private medical coverage immediately but within a few months were able to build this into our plans too. The group scheme costs remain significantly better value than for individuals, and so it was a relatively low cost to absorb for the business. This benefit had become relatively standard for large companies and offering this same benefit as a small company made a statement to prospective employees.

Commercial risks

Whilst insurance can resolve some of your risk issues it cannot offset all of them. Possibly the greatest risk for a new business is that you do not get all your planning assumptions right, which can lead to a difference in your profitability in the early months. This could clearly result in either an over or under performance versus plan. In either event, it is in your interest to have as much flexibility in your costs to be able to make changes as you become more certain about your actual performance levels. This is, of course, especially important if your performance is behind the plan; by limiting your commitments and maintaining as much flexibility as possible you are increasing your ability to rectify your model.

This may mean that you are paying a little more for some services in the short term but it may be better to accept this extra cost than risk a long-term contract that might not fit your needs in a few months. Examples include:

- renting company vehicles
- flexible phone contracts
- business premises with a short-term arrangement.

TIP There are many small business centres now on the market providing cost effective space and/or the ability to share other facilities such as conference rooms, display equipment and the like. They often also provide a stimulating environment with other new start-ups to share experiences with. Search for options in your local area – you will be surprised at the choice.

The same principle applies to other areas of your business operation. We will discuss in more detail in Part 3 the merits of outsourcing functions. This can be a very effective way of getting the tasks performed that you need without hiring staff. Recruiting permanent employees is not only time consuming but pertains to a longer term commitment that you should not enter into until you have confidence that the business model is holding up.

Short-term contracts will generally get you through those first few tentative months when you are in the process of proving to yourself and others that your business plan can work. You can proceed with more confidence once you have got through that critical first phase.

Maintaining your flexibility in the early days is an important way of managing your commercial risk. Spend time thinking about all your contacts and how they might be able to help you. Do not be afraid either to beg, borrow or steal resource to help you start up; whether this is a desk in an office, or use of equipment, or some unpaid help from former colleagues or friends. Anything that cuts your costs and reduces commitment is a powerful ally in your quest to minimise the risk of starting up.

It can also make sense to build in a formal contingency into your financial plan as an extra cost line. This might be based on a small percentage of sales, or just a fixed amount, but it helps demonstrate some prudence to your stakeholders and gives you a nice little cushion that can help "pay for" any nasty surprise that suddenly would otherwise have an adverse effect on your financial performance.

Customers and suppliers

If you find it difficult to predict elements of your own business plan, then predicting the performance of other businesses that you deal with will be even harder. How your customers and suppliers behave can be very unpredictable.

A business can reduce risk by having as broad a spread of customers and suppliers as is feasible for their type of activity. No one customer or supplier can then have a large impact on the business. This may not be possible for many reasons, e.g. a consultancy can usually only operate with a limited number of customers. You may never be able to eliminate the risk that a key client walks away leaving a big hole in your income stream, but you can manage this risk by ensuring that you can quickly change your cost base to mirror the income reduction.

In addition to losing an income stream, the other major financial risk to be aware of is the unexpected inability of a customer to pay for goods supplied – bad debt. This will affect all businesses and there are a number of ways to deal with it. There are insurance options available but of course at a cost. The best way of managing this risk is to only trade with reputable customers, but if you have concerns make sure that the potential exposure is limited. Alas, with the best will and crystal ball you will still have problems from time to time. Making a provision in your accounts for some level of bad debt is the wisest option. This means that you do not have to worry so much about any individual situation as long as you have provided prudently.

Contracts

The very word "contract" makes you think about picking up the phone and calling a lawyer, but in reality they can be simpler or more complicated all at the same time. Any working relationship you have begins to form a contract irrespective of whether anything is written down, as the legal system deems that established practice can of itself create a contractual relationship between two parties. The same applies to oral contracts; if you have said you will do something you run the risk of being arguably liable to perform your promise.

As we have already suggested, there are some aspects of your activities you will want to ensure do not commit you for other than the short term. But, on the other hand, if you can negotiate longer term contractual commitments with customers or key suppliers then they may be very advantageous to your venture.

The first formal "contracts" you will probably need to give thought to are the employment contracts with your employees and secondly your standard trading terms and conditions. Formal employment contracts are now a legal requirement, but they do not need to be complex and there are many sources of examples online that you can personalise for your own situation. Similarly, you should have a standard set of trading terms and conditions which form part of the invoice (often written on the back) which include things like your payment terms, returns procedure and similar aspects relevant to the provision of your goods or service to the customer. Again, you can create these yourself – often by looking at other business invoices that are in a similar trade to your own (even your former employer!). A cross-check against some standard templates on the internet should mean you are confident enough to produce these without needing formal legal advice, and a final tip would be to ask your bank to look at your proposed set for you.

Some aspects of your business will sooner or later require a more detailed formalised contract, and a general rule might be that if the other party is using legal services to prepare or negotiate the contract then you probably need to do so too. It is important to remember a few key things about any contract, whether its formally written or just a simple trade transaction governed by oral and written communications:

- Only agree to perform tasks that you know you can complete.
- Agree a length of arrangement that suits your needs.
- Make sure it does not restrict you in any undesirable way (e.g. from trading with other customers, or to pass on necessary price increases).
- Consider all the terms carefully.
- Contracts that are fair to both parties promote a better relationship and long-term two-way loyalty.

Finally, remember that any simple purchase is in reality creating a contract between you and the supplier, so taking care is paramount. One simple example caused much amusement amongst the rank and file at Ubevco but illustrates the point.

We were lucky one year to have both a Rugby and Cricket World Cup played in the UK, and one of our beers, Castle Lager, were the sponsors of the South Africa team favoured to do well in both events. Dennis, as Managing Director, decided to take a hands on role in ensuring we had good marketing presence at all the South Africa matches (including his own in a spectator seat). Somehow the parasols he wanted had been missed off the initial order of display materials, so he personally ordered these to be flown over from Cape Town rather than use the normal cheaper sea freight. Now that would have been fine, except he didn't consider the small print and the 100 relatively small and light parasols were accompanied

by 100 big round concrete support stands – which were duly air freighted as well. The bill was astronomical but the mileage we got from telling the story at the venues was an unexpected marketing benefit in itself!

Your ambition

We applaud ambition and without it you are unlikely to want to run your own business. However, our own ambitions and ego can sometimes bring with them additional risk. You will be enthusiastic, of course, about your new venture and your core proposition, but it is all too common for entrepreneurs to become over optimistic about how quickly and easily their new idea will take over the world.

Perhaps it is better to call it over optimism, but the real message here is that you need a base plan that is prudent, that assumes that things might be a bit slower to start than you might wish and you will get some hiccups along the way. If you over achieve this plan significantly, you will have a wonderful problem to deal with. The flexibility that you have built into your model will equally allow you to scale up easily.

Health and safety

In the context of discussing risk assessment, we should mention that it is now a legal requirement for any business with employees to perform a formal risk assessment of the hazards in your business and to take practical steps to reduce the risk of accidents in the workplace. There is plenty of on-line help to ensure that you not only comply with the legalities but also take the right steps to effect this reduction in risk. At the time of writing, the government is proposing making smaller enterprises exempt from some of the existing requirements, but check thoroughly to make sure you meet all your responsibilities.

The Health and Safety Executive's website is a good source of guidance: www.hse.gov.uk

Personal guarantees

Minimising the risks within your business before and as you start will clearly help reduce the risks to your own financial status, but there is one area of overlap that merits particular attention, that of the "personal guarantee".

Our dear friends in the banking community love personal guarantees. They will justify asking you for a personal guarantee as additional security to support a business loan on the grounds that it demonstrates your personal belief and commitment to the venture. It is hard to argue against that sentiment, but what they also want is to be able to rely on any equity in your home or personal assets to fall back on if your business fails.

When negotiating with your bankers it may not be possible to eliminate the need for giving some guarantee but if you do so we would strongly advise that you do not make it open-ended. Some or all of the following conditions will help manage your risk:

- Limit the amount of the personal guarantee to a smaller precise sum rather than the full amount of any loan.
- Seek to negotiate a strict time limit on how long the guarantee remains in place.
- Ask for automatic removal once certain performance criteria are met.
- Make the guarantee specific to an agreed facility. It is very easy to sign up to a personal guarantee for an initial small loan, then forget about it and some years later when your business has changed complexity find you are guaranteeing a different level of facility all together.

If you have business partners, guarantees are usually joint and several. This can mean you end up guaranteeing the entire loan not just your share. Families can easily get sucked into personal-guarantee situations, either as provider or cross guarantor or just in the fall out when things go wrong.

Often the bad stories you hear about are the ramifications of a personal guarantee being called upon are when the situation has run for some years and the parties have not retained awareness of the risk and current status. So if you sign one, stay on top of its terms and risks and negotiate them hard.

In Summary

The key message in this chapter is to start up in such a way that if you need to make changes to your model, the financial impact on you is limited.

There are many factors that may be entirely outside of your control that can harm your fledgling business. You may suddenly find that you are undercut in the market, or new competitors enter your market, or the market for your product or service undergoes some unforeseen change. Hopefully, you will have considered these risks as part of your overall conceptualisation of your proposition and strategy, and that the likelihood of these happening is remote.

Sometimes though, things might just conspire against you no matter how well you have planned your business. Understanding what the risks are and how you can manage your business around them is sensible if not essential. So you will find it helpful to:

- Consult a specialised business insurance broker to help you assess your insurance needs.
- In the early days, keep your financial commitments low and your flexibility high to allow you to confirm the key elements of your financial plan.
- Make a provision for some bad debts and don't overexpose yourself to any single one.
- Be ambitious and financially prudent – the two are mutually compatible.
- If you have to give a personal guarantee to your bank, ensure that there are strict criteria that will allow you to remove it at the earliest possible time.
- Be aware of your need for formal contracts and ensure you understand the detail.

Chapter 11

The final plan and how to use it

All the topics in the book so far have covered all the key issues and the thinking you need to go through to produce your *final business plan*. The production of a formal documented plan is an important step particularly to engage the stakeholders in your business. A stakeholder is the formal name for any individual or organisation that is affected by the activities of your business. It therefore encompasses investors, bankers, your main suppliers, customers, employees and maybe even your family. Whatever your circumstances, you will need the support of some or all of these stakeholders.

If your stakeholders do not have confidence in your venture it is likely to be more difficult for you to achieve your goals. You will need to think about how they will view your decisions throughout your business life but during your start-up period it is particularly important.

The best way to influence them in the early days is through having a compelling business plan.

The business plan

A quick internet search will soon offer any number of suggested formats and templates from which you can choose for writing up your business plan. In the main they cover the same core areas.

For you though, this is now more a process of setting everything down in a single document. As we have already covered in the earlier chapters, you have already been through most of the thought processes you need to go through to address the main topics. It is very important that your thinking influences your business plan and not the other way round. For some new businesses the first time they really start to join up their thinking is when they are trying to fill in the boxes of the plan.

Typical contents of a business plan

Executive summary – this briefly summarises the key points of the various sections below with the aim of interesting the reader sufficiently to explore the detail.

Business Description – in Chapters 3 and 5 we have worked through the process of setting out your core proposition and goals, which would typically be summarised here.

Market background – in Chapter 3 we suggested that by looking around and looking ahead you would establish that there is an opportunity for you to provide a product or service for a particular market given the conditions you have observed. Further in Chapter 5 we explored the external factors that firm up your idea. You would explain all these findings here.

Service and operational details – when developing the core idea into a meaningful proposition in Chapter 5, we discussed the internal factors relevant to your business and whether you can execute the actual process. Here you need to provide the same comfort that you can operationally provide the goods and services efficiently.

Marketing and sales strategy – you should provide a broad outline of the strategy you will employ to market your product/ service and how you will execute sales. The thought processes here formed part of the overall business concept development in Chapters 3 and 5. You should also include how you plan to brand the business itself as discussed in Chapter 9.

Management and organisation – this should set out the credentials of the management team and a summary of your proposed organisation structure. We outlined the structural options in Chapter 8 and debated the merits of external advisers in Chapter 7.

Financial plan – the details of the processes we discussed in Chapter 6 to produce your budget, which will show detail for at least 12 months and outline for probably three years.

Risk analysis – it is sometimes helpful to set out any key risk factors that you have identified as pertinent to your business. Illustrating an awareness of these, and how you propose managing the risks as discussed in Chapter 10, is particularly important when presenting the plan to bankers or investors.

The business plan can and should be edited according to your audience. If for instance you are presenting to a potential lender then you should make clear how they will be repaid whereas if you are presenting to a potential investor, they will be more interested in where and when he might get a return. An emphasis on this and mention in the executive summary, therefore, would be sensible.

A shorter more focused version might be suitable for presenting to other key people you need to support the business. This might include your insurers, key suppliers, and even customers. The business plan really at this stage acts as a credentials presentation, but sharing your goals and vision for the business can generally only be a positive interaction with future business associates.

We also suggest sharing the plan with employees, which may seem like an obvious thing to do but is still by no means the norm. Of course, there may be some sensitive information therein which it is not just practical or desirable to share with prospective employees, but this is easily dealt with through judicious editing.

In general terms though, the same key aspects are likely to impress your stakeholders:

- a convincing core proposition
- sensible goals
- a clear strategy
- a sound financial plan
- realism and proper risk assessment
- your experience
- associations with advisors or mentors
- your investors
- your commitment.

All these key factors should have emerged from thought processes you have been through, which emphasises that the formal document itself is just a summary of all your planning.

If your business plan fails to influence the desired stakeholder positively this probably points to flaws and you need to take heed. Essentially, for whatever the reason, you have failed to convince the other party that your business will succeed.

Ensure that you do not create the wrong impression through making schoolboy errors such as:

- poor or careless presentation
- simple errors
- over optimistic claims or goals.

The best plans combine confidence and enthusiasm with a heavy dose of realism. As you are using the business plan to influence people it is worth giving some thought to presentation. Take the opportunity to make it look professional, as this will affect the way it is perceived. Think about the presentation in the context of your business branding – it is an opportunity to make the plan look very much part of your business, including logos, relevant typeface and colours.

TIPS

- Format your business plan to suit your business and your needs; do not slavishly follow someone else's format.
- Keep the content clear and concise.
- Avoid errors.
- Tailor it for different stakeholder groups.
- Give it some standout through presentation.

Stakeholders influencing stakeholders

Gaining the confidence of your potential stakeholders is a vital step forward in getting your business started. You will find that the higher the confidence that your stakeholder has, the better the results will be whether it be the bank facility, the lines of credit from your suppliers, the commerciality of your buying terms, the willingness of your customers to buy, etc.

Additionally, stakeholders gain confidence from each other. If they see the involvement of an individual or organisation that they trust, then that breeds more confidence in you. This is one of the reasons that so many new ventures will try and enlist the support of an established business expert as an investor, mentor or non-executive director. The right person can definitely add credence to your offering as well as providing expertise in specific areas where you own knowledge may be lacking.

This power of positive association will continue as you start trading. If, for example, you can gain the custom of an established and well-respected organisation, other businesses will notice and take you more seriously.

In summary

The formalisation of your business plan into a document that can be presented to stakeholders represents the end of the conceptualisation and planning phase of your new venture. We have tried to cover all the key thought processes through the first two parts of this book. Your business plan should be a simple and comprehensive explanation of your business proposition, strategy and financial plan.

- Tailor the content so that it is relevant for your different stakeholder groups.
- It should look good.
- Be clear and accurate.

Your business plan is a concise summary of your business vision and financial plan. If done well, it can be a very powerful tool, which you can utilise in many situations to help instil confidence in your new venture.

It signifies that you are done with the thinking and it's time to start putting your plans into action.

PART 3

THE NUTS AND BOLTS OF RUNNING YOUR BUSINESS

Once all the pieces of your business puzzle have been fitted together, you will have a clear picture of your new venture. This is the really exciting time where you move from the planning stage to the actual execution of your ideas and vision.

In Part 3, we are going to address some of the key issues that relate to the everyday workings of a new company. In the first three chapters we will discuss the things you need to put in place straight away to ensure that you will make the business secure, including:

- Thinking about how to organise and manage your business using processes and outsourcing under the premise of "keeping things simple".
- Creating the working environment to best suit you whilst at the same time generating a motivating business ethos for everyone working with you.
- As the business settles, the day-to-day working of the business will normalise. It is important though that you keep your strategy on track as circumstances change and evolve. This will also be the time to ensure that the business that you have created is working the way you want it to.

We will then start to discuss some of the issues that will affect the business as you start to establish yourself and need to start thinking about the longer term, including:

- Creating and managing strong relationships both inside and outside of your company will become ever more important. We also address ways to manage conflict when it occurs.
- As your business begins to succeed, you will hopefully start to grow. Growth can bring with it another set of issues to deal with. We will discuss how to plan for growth.
- Finally, we will highlight the issue of change management. It affects most businesses at some point and requires a specific set of tools to manage effectively.

Chapter **12**

Working smartly

If you have put the time and effort into your planning process, producing simple and focused planning systems, you are ready to extend this philosophy into the day-to-day organisation of your company.

Keeping it simple

The precise way in which you manage your business will depend on the nature of your undertaking and the size of your operation in terms of people, customers, suppliers and turnover. Whatever the size and structure the key is to keep things simple. If you do not keep your business and the way you operate it simple, then you will get distracted from the things you are best at; indeed the very things you have planned to be the income drivers of your venture.

If your business demonstrates it is very good at doing its core activity, it will succeed and grow. You can always add the second and third strings to your bow later if you have exhausted the possibilities of this core activity, and have support around you to make all three work.

To enable you to focus on your key skill, try to make all the elements around managing your business as simple as possible.

Simple processes

The benefits of simple processes can be summarised as:

- time saving
- easier to understand
- easier to perform
- less likely to result in human error
- less likely to fail (computer glitches and similar)
- usually cheaper.

These benefits can apply to many of the different processes you will be involved in. It does not matter that they are unsophisticated nor using the leading edge technology, the objective is to make sure that the processes do the basic job and allow you to focus on delivering your priority objective.

For instance, many of your administrative and record keeping tasks can be maintained using standard spreadsheets rather than using specialised software. As part of your planning you may have already put some basic tracking devices into place.

Setting yourself some basic routines and disciplines can also help build an efficient working platform for your organisation. If there are several of you involved in the management of your business, a short regular "action meeting" is a great discipline for planning both the immediate and longer-term priorities and tasks that need to be performed. Even if you are on your own, a regular allotted time to produce your weekly "to do" list is a simple but effective tool to help you manage your affairs.

The IT revolution means that we now have a surfeit of information flow. If anything it is humans that are the limiting factor as we tend to be only able to focus on a few key things. IT systems that are cost effective, reliable and focused on the core task are often more appropriate than over sophisticated versions that take too long to install for too much money.

> At Ubevco, Dennis used to read all the invoices before they were mailed out, not because he couldn't get a report with the same data on, but because it helped him focus on what the data meant and made him think about each customer as he went through them. He found it was much easier to absorb what was happening than reading a computer report.

Simple and focused management

The notion of keeping things simple should not just be confined to the processes within your business. As we touched upon in Chapter 8:

- The way you set up the enterprise, whether it is a limited company, partnership or sole trader, should also strive to be simple.
- Similarly, the financial arrangements between shareholders, how profits are shared, where relevant, will all benefit by being straightforward.

This equally applies to how you pay any employees, how they earn bonuses and how their terms and conditions are structured. If they are simply structured, there is much better understanding and any bonus element will become much more effective as a tool for driving better performance. We will discuss remuneration matters further in Chapter 15.

> We used two simple reports in the business with great effect.
>
> Firstly, we had the daily sales report that was issued every evening showing the sales that day, the sales for the month to date and a straight-line projection for the months end. This focused everyone on the gap between the sales achieved so far and what we needed to sell by the end of the month. See example in Chapter 6.
>
> Secondly, we had a twelve-month sales forecast, which was updated each month. This showed sales by brand and was created from inputs from sales, marketing and logistics. In theory, therefore, everyone owned it. It was important because it was the one report that everyone worked from and was also used to feed into the company financial plan at a higher level. Again, it was created as a simple excel spreadsheet and did not use any sort of extrapolations or complicated equations. It reported actual numbers and clearly showed where we were performing on target and where we had issues. It facilitated conversations about action required to deliver the plans.

Simple priorities

Lastly, the keeping-it-simple philosophy can apply equally well to the core activity and priorities. If you set very focused objectives and are successful at achieving them, you will set up a platform and confidence both internally and externally to allow you to progress to much broader objectives in the future.

> We have tried to launch new drinks into the UK market on many occasions. Our strategy was usually the same – see if you can make the product work somewhere with

a simple and focused approach. This frequently involved just selling it in one particular geographic area, a city or a part of a city. Alternatively, we might target just one type of customer or outlet. So for instance when introducing a new soft drink, we might focus on London sandwich bars within the W1 postcode area.

This approach enables you to really attack one fragment of the market and demonstrate to yourself and the consumers in that market that your product works.

This can apply to service industries as well. The aim is the same, focus your attention on a particular part of the market and you are much more likely to succeed and learn about how best to develop your sales in other markets.

This may seem obvious and over simplistic but too many businesses try to be over ambitious and spread themselves and their thinking far too thin in the early days before they have established a strong financial base for the business.

We are in no doubt that we were able to succeed in our business because we kept things very simple, even when we were turning over in excess of £100 m with 130 employees. We tried to maintain simplicity in our processes and focus in our core objectives and ensured that this culture was embraced all the way through our organisation.

Outsourcing key functions

"Outsourcing is the process of contracting a business function to someone else. It is sometimes confused with offshoring, though a function may be outsourced without offshoring or vice versa."
Wikipedia

For any young business, outsourcing key functions is a vital tool. It enables you to:

- focus on your strengths and the core part of your business plan;
- minimise risk; and
- benefit from some economies of scale that bigger corporations are able to generate.

For virtually every function it would be possible to outsource but clearly if you are to develop a successful business with its own identity, you need to perform the primary functions for which you are to become known. The competitive advantage that you should be striving to achieve lies in the core activity and that is where your focus should remain.

The type of key functions that are usually best outsourced will vary according to the type of business you are operating, but let's start with perhaps the easiest and most frequently used example, the payroll service.

Virtually all small and medium-sized businesses that have more than a couple of employees will be using an outsourced payroll service. For a small fee, a provider will produce for you the entire monthly and annual payroll data you are required to provide to your employees and the tax authorities. All you do is submit any changes or temporary adjustments each month (such as overtime, bonus, or change in tax code) and they will use their specialised software systems and stationery to produce the necessary documents. You can do this yourself but the software, stationery and particularly time costs you will incur do not compare to the price at which these specialist companies provide the same service. Many were originally owned by or connected with the leading banks, but there is also a wide choice of independent suppliers.

We found that with some judicious outsourcing, more than one benefit could arise from a single outsource operator. Two major outsourced functions were critical to the success of our business and particularly their ability to cope with the dramatic growth we experienced.

1 Factoring or invoice discounting

For many smaller businesses, the easiest way to finance their business is through factoring, or it's near neighbour invoice discounting. These types of facility used to enjoy something of a mixed reputation when they first started being used by UK businesses. There was a perception that it was the last resort available to a business when traditional sources of bank finance had been refused. This is a misplaced view.

The principle is quite simple. With factoring, you effectively sell your debtors to the bank (or other factor provider), so that each time you raise invoices to customers, the bank buys them from you and advances you an agreed percentage (normally somewhere around 70%) of the invoice value that very same day. The invoice will be marked to show that you have sold the invoice to the bank instructing the customer to pay the bank rather than your business.

So if you sold £10,000 of invoiced items on Monday, you would send the details to the bank and they would give you £7,000. When the customer pays the invoice to the bank you get the remaining £3,000. You will pay a small fee to the factoring bank. The bank is responsible for collecting the money from your customer and so performs that function for you.

Invoice discounting operates under the same principle with regard to the advancing of monies against invoices, but is more discrete. The customer still pays you direct rather than the bank, and you retain responsibility for chasing the customers for payment. Your customer may have no idea that you are discounting your invoices. Typically though, banks will only consider invoice discounting for larger and well established companies, as it requires a higher level of trust and robust IT systems that can cope easily with the daily flow of information needed to enable them to monitor the position.

For Ubevco it was by far the best form of finance available and over the next decade allowed the business to expand and contract its turnover and lending needs relatively seamlessly. This mechanism framed how we negotiated terms with key suppliers and gave us the confidence that we could fund the business. There were two big added benefits to using factoring:

- The bank rather than Ubevco would handle chasing the customers for money, thereby relieving us of the need to hire a resource ourselves for this.
- The facility also provided credit insurance against a customer going bankrupt.

We have, and will again, labour the point that as a basic principle any company should look to minimise the risk of incurring bad debts.

Of course, you pay for such a service, but even as our business grew to over £100m turnover, the combination of these services was still more cost effective than trying to source them individually or internally. In fact, only a banking facility as flexible as factoring could have coped with the growth of facility needed to allow our turnover to rise so rapidly.

The Asset Based Finance Association (ABFA) maintains a list of providers together with details of any turnover requirements they may have and details of the services they can offer. As with most financial products, there are many variations of the core facility available which might suit your particular business and circumstances (www.abfa.org.uk).

2 Logistics

Our business imported products that needed storing until we could sell them. They were bulky, needed to have excise duty paid on them and required delivery throughout the UK. We had set up our business in a matter of days to take advantage of the particular situation we found ourselves in. We therefore had little option but to outsource the logistical process to third party suppliers, but it was in any case the best choice.

Throughout the entire life of our business, all our products were stored with third party warehouse and haulage companies; we never owned a truck, hired a driver or indeed even set eyes on the products we sold other than the ones in our office fridge. This meant we could cope with our exceptional growth (and subsequent decline!) both through the ability of our existing providers to absorb the growth and by adding further suppliers and depots. We can only imagine how limited our growth would have been had we had to operate our own warehousing, or how financially crippling had we bought a warehouse prior to losing the contract to sell Red Bull.

The use of outsourcing does not mean you can just sit back and pay no attention to the service you are receiving, particularly when the outsourcer is interacting with customers, suppliers or employees. The outsource company is, in effect, your representative and you should take some responsibility for ensuring they are performing well. As part of the service agreement you enter into, you should agree specific standards of service. In the logistics example, it might be that you will provide orders by email each day by a specified time and they will deliver them within a certain time period according to geographic location.

You need to protect your business from being overexposed to a situation where a key outsourced supplier suddenly fails to provide an adequate service. The reputation of your business can be tarnished just as easily by the outsourcer as by your own actions.

One of the higher profile cases of outsourcing problems in recent years concerned Railtrack, whose decision to outsource nearly all its track maintenance has been criticised on the basis that as a core activity of the business it should have been conducted from within. Track issues were contributory factors in separate accidents during the period of 1997–2000, and there was concern not just about the decision to outsource, but the way that outsourcers were managed.

Criticisms were voiced on a number of issues. It was said that the outsource companies were themselves using sub-contractors and the overall project was not managed properly with adequate communications, documented systems and working procedures.

Finally, some commentators questioned whether appropriate service level agreements had been set and whether the chosen vendors actually had the necessary expertise to undertake the required functions.

Whilst this example is on a very large scale, all these principles apply equally to a small business when considering whether to use an outsource provider. Time and cost are probably the primary drivers that lead you towards considering using one but make sure you cover all the related issues and concerns.

TIPS FOR SUCCESSFUL OUTSOURCING

- Make expectations clear and part of your formal agreement.
- Perform some due diligence to ensure they can do the job.
- Take up references, both financial and operational.
- Ensure that arrangements are mutually beneficial and not one sided.
- Consider split sources if possible, but make that policy clear to all parties.
- Monitor and manage supplier performance.
- Communicate on an ongoing basis.
- Share problems and opportunities and work together for best solutions.
- Try and pick suppliers that fit your style.

Any web search browse of the term "outsource" will demonstrate that the term has become widely associated with two particular aspects: the provision of IT services by external providers and the use of low cost international call centres. For some reason, business literature seems to forget the fact that many long established companies utilise outsourcing for the very basic and essential functions of manufacturing their product and delivering it to their customers. These are classic examples of effective outsourcing.

During our time working with Red Bull, when they were still in the process of establishing the brand, they outsourced all their manufacturing and their relatively small head office in Austria concentrated on what they perceived as their core activities, the sales and marketing of their brand which clearly underpinned their success. Despite incredible growth, we never had a single supply problem or product-quality issue.

Clearly, production is very important, and when such a vital process of your business is to be outsourced you should consider multiple providers to protect from a failure in service provision by one such provider. This is hard to do when you are a small company, where your scale of business does not merit splitting between providers, but you should give thought as soon as you can to this principle.

Whilst all our factoring and debt collection in Ubevco was performed by one bank, we did also open up an active trading relationship with another bank. This not only gave us somewhere else to go should the service with our factor provider fail or we should fall out with them, it also enabled us to get better terms. The second bank would always be keen to quote for our main factor business and the quotes we got helped us negotiate improved rates from our existing provider. So the use of multiple providers gave us both protection and competition to the advantage of our business.

We did exactly the same with other key functions, using three different warehousing and transport firms to store and deliver our products to customers. The policy was proved when one of the providers suddenly started missing promised delivery times and causing customer service problems. This resulted from them taking on some other new business, whilst at the same time, making system changes and for a few weeks they could not cope. We were able to switch away business to one of our other logistics providers for a few weeks whilst they rectified the problems. It pleased everyone, customer service returned to normal and we helped what had otherwise been a good supplier to overcome a temporary problem as good business partners should do.

The internet age has undoubtedly increased the trend for businesses to outsource, particularly in areas such as HR management and IT where smaller companies do not have the scale to justify specialist employees to perform these tasks. These companies offer ancillary services such as employee expense management and even sickness control. The employee has to phone the HR provider to explain their symptoms if they are reporting sick. The argument is that this works as a deterrent for the employee who might be fancying an extra day off work, yet by being done remotely doesn't threaten the employer–employee trust relationship. You can make your own mind up on this. Our view would be try to have motivated employees who like going to work and save on the HR service.

As you grow, you should keep under constant review whether some of your outsourced tasks can be brought in house. Certain functions are more likely to be performed by outsourcing and probably physical product delivery is the best example. Even the largest companies outsource this part of their business rather than own and manage fleets of lorries or ships.

In the early days, we used outsourced support for the day to day management of our IT, things like hardware failures, installations, upgrades and similar routine maintenance and development. But as we grew we waited far too long to bring in our own dedicated IT manager and when we did it halved our cost yet created extra resource to take advantage of the technological developments of the day. The same can be said of human resource management for many businesses. In our experience, once you move into the range of having 40–60 employees, both of these functions are better performed in house with your own employee.

Why did we wait so long to bring our IT function in house? Well, the conspiracy theorists suggest that it was because outsource company used to bring pizzas into the office for general consumption every Tuesday and as word got around it was surprising how many of the sales team popped into the office to have their PC checked over on Tuesday lunchtime. Things changed though when one Christmas time, the pizzas brought in were laden with brussel sprouts. A very unpopular move and the new IT manager was soon to follow.

What is hard to comprehend (especially for many consumers) is the trend of the last decade to outsource call centre functions – usually to a far-flung country – on the grounds that the average cost of handling of a call is a fraction of the cost. Yet, what they fail to grasp is that for many of their customers the only contact they ever have with their company is through this call centre, and that representation is so frequently below an acceptable standard through lack of product knowledge, language and dialect or waiting/connection issues. There should be a wall of shame created to highlight which CEOs allowed their company to be taken down this path on their watch! The lesson is that outsourcing of any type can affect the quality of your business offering.

However, you may have the need for phone-answering services yourself and all will be well and good, provided you brief the receptionists properly and regularly do some quality control checks yourself.

It is hard to envisage any business that does not need to utilise some outsourcing. Deciding which parts of the operation would benefit from using it and then managing the outsourcers can be very important to the success of your business, and should not be underestimated. Certain activities such as logistics, physical production and payroll may always be better outsourced, whereas others may be better switched back in house over time. The right combination of each will vary according to your own particular business activity and circumstances.

In summary

In this chapter we have urged you to give yourself the very best chance of succeeding by focusing as much of your time as possible on delivering excellence in your core activity.

To do so, organise your operations very simply:

- Use outsourcing where appropriate; you will free up your time to achieve this.
- Monitor the services that you outsource to ensure that you receive a quality service.

Chapter **13**

The right environment

Organising the business so it is effective is essential as it underpins your ability to be profitable. It is important also to remember that one reason for leaving employment is your desire to enjoy work more. A key benefit of running your own business is that you have the opportunity to influence the ambiance of the business; everything from the layout of your premises to the underlying moral principles that govern day-to-day business practice.

Working in the right environment will enhance the experience for you greatly, irrespective of the type of company you are in and the number of people you work with. Job satisfaction is made up a variety of factors including the environment we experience within the organisation.

Establishing the right physical environment whether it is office space, a shop, a warehouse or a production line is important but often the easier part of the equation. More difficult is the company culture, which will affect the way we feel and behave about those around us. The culture of a business is important, as it will affect both the internal operation of your organisation and the external impression of it.

The physical environment

Do not underestimate the importance of your physical surroundings. If you have been working in a large corporation, you may well have been used to high value premises with all the luxuries you could wish for. You are not going to be able to compete with that in the early days. What is important is that your physical environment whether it is an office, an industrial unit,or space in your home, is practical, affordable and comfortable for you and anyone working with you.

Working from home is an interesting option for many. It offers a number of advantages: literally no travel time (unless you have to walk down to the garden to the shed!), it is low cost and in the early days can offer the flexibility you need as you establish the business. However, there can be a downside, as you have no separation between home and work life and the impact on your family needs to be considered.

Sharing office space is another way of keeping your costs down. There are many offices set up to offer this service where you can share such things as receptionist services, IT facilities, etc. The advantage of this route is the flexibility it gives you – you can expand your space as you need to – and the professionalism of the environment. You often find other young businesses sharing the offices and the ambience can be very supportive. You will need to explore the availability of such facilities locally.

Finally, you can choose to literally rent desk space or meeting rooms, as you need them. Regus is the big national operator in this area. The cost per hour is not particularly cheap but it is cost efficient in that you only use them when you need them. We sometimes use these facilities in our consultancy business; most of the time we can work most effectively from home but if we need to set up a client meeting in a more formal environment the Regus option works well for us.

Of course, your business may well dictate where you are located and the type of premises you must have. It is important to try and keep your costs both low and flexible in the early days whilst creating a strong working environment appropriate for your business.

There are some simple things that do not cost very much that can make a real difference:

- *Location – you get to choose this*. Reducing or even eradicating your travel time to work will just add value to your business – you can work in this previously dead time.
- *Make it look professional.* The adage "first impressions are lasting impressions" is sadly true. So anyone visiting your business should be presented with a smart first impression. Sometimes this can be easily dealt with in a reception area. Making it clean and welcoming will cost you little but effort.
- *Make your workspace efficient for those that use it*. You have the opportunity as you start your business to make sure it works practically to best effect. Organise your space to be efficient as this will make it easier to work in. Think about where the office equipment is placed in the context of those that use it; make it ergonomically work.
- *Make it comfortable*. It is very easy to offer home comforts cheaply – tea and coffee that is not out of a machine is a simple but great benefit in the small company.

- *Make it presentable for those who work there.* If you allow the workspace to be a mess, then it probably will be a mess. No one cares about their work space like they care about their home space but if you ask for the space to be kept tidy, everyone will benefit. And, of course, you need to lead by example.

> The office space we chose was open plan and a largely blank canvas but importantly was affordable.
>
> We managed our costs by popping down to Ikea and purchasing our furniture and this brought the additional advantage of a new skill – assembling desks, chairs, bookcases, filing cabinets, etc. This allowed us to afford a reasonable quality with a contemporary image.
>
> This furniture stood the test of time and much of it survived the life of the company. As we grew and money became less of an issue, the first thing we did was to invest in a smart reception area including a large bespoke piece of glass etched with our company and brand logos. This created a smart first impression for visitors to the business. Most never knew that behind it lurked a good impression of an Ikea showroom!

The business culture

In simple terms, culture is a shared system of understanding, influencing how we behave and what we value. It is the glue that binds a group together, the group DNA. Culture defines the way in which a group of people solve problems and resolve dilemmas – which at the end of the day is what we have to do every day in business.

One potential danger is that we define the organisation in terms of what we don't want. There are many things culturally about corporate life that we may not like – the politics, the layers of hierarchy and ensuing bureaucracy, being kept in the dark, to name but a few – but to be successful it is important that the expression of your culture be both positive and cohesive. In that way, members of the organisation will be able to buy into the vision.

If you are essentially a one-person operation, it is not really necessary to think about managing the culture of your business, as you will instinctively work according to your own principles and values. But even if you are working with a small team, it is worth giving some thought to the ethos of the business; if you do not take the lead, it is quite possible that those around you will dictate it for you.

Things to think about:

1 If you can, try to express the values you want to see:

- Think about what is important to you and to the success of the business. You need to be able to explain this to others.
- Think about your core proposition – what is it about your business that is different and what will you need to do to achieve that point of difference? This will include some elements that are about the physical organisation and other elements that are about the way in which you behave to achieve them, i.e. the values, attributes and behaviours that will be important. This can be especially relevant to areas such as customer service teams.
- Try and do this early on and then share it with those around you. You can evolve and improve it over time.

2 Make sure that any outward signs of your culture are strong, including:

- Any logos, branding, shop signage. As we discussed in "business branding", any form of company branding is sending a message about you and so you need to think about the sort of message you want to give.
- The organisation structure – reporting systems, pay structures, etc. Typically, these define hierarchies, team structure and generally affect the way people relate to each other. If you wish to develop a culture where people are independent and able to use their initiative, then a highly structured reporting system may not be the most appropriate. Whereas, if you need the organisation to be highly efficient and process led, then how you organise and incentivise would be different.

- In large corporations you often see departments and functions organised in very insular ways, which means each works to a different business agenda. This can be very damaging in the smaller business where usually you need everyone very focused on the same objectives. Think about how you can best engender this in your company through such things as structure and pay policy.

3 Keep it real:

- Make sure that everything that you do as a leader of the business is consistent with the values that you have – lead by example.
- Look at how you can practically build in the cultural values in the following areas:
  - recruitment
  - training and development
  - reward structures
  - team building
  - do things that allow you to build the company spirit, for example, company events, meetings, social occasions, which can bring everyone together to great effect.
  - "Live the culture". Do not be afraid to reference the culture to those around you. In simple terms, people often refer to "work hard, play hard" as a particular feature of their work environment. In itself this is a simplistic statement of culture but even so it states what unites the members of the organisation. Think about the things that can unite your company.

4 Avoid corporate pitfalls!

- You may have an idea of what you want it to be but, in reality, it will take time to establish, so give it time to develop. As the business leader, you can watch for the less healthy elements you may identify with in corporate life and deal with them accordingly. Manage the culture don't let it manage you.

- Don't recruit clones! An easy mistake when you are applying criteria into an interview situation. Look at values not personalities – there is a difference.
- Don't underestimate the value of experience. You can benefit from more than your own years of experience in corporate life. You may be able to recruit and benefit from very experienced individuals in all areas of the business. Although the majority of our sales team may have been relatively young, we also had some seasoned individuals who were nearing retirement age doing the same job bringing the benefit of experience to everyone in the team.

The Ubevco way

In the early days, the long-term culture of our organisation didn't register as a business issue.

We were careful to create the right office environment. It was important to us that everyone worked together well. We created an open plan office that encouraged discussion between all functions and discouraged the development of unnecessary hierarchies. We wanted to create the right ambience to encourage a strong team spirit.

After the first couple of years, there was a slow emerging awareness of culture; people started to say things like 'that's not the Ubevco way'. There was an awareness that we did things a certain way and that this was an important factor where we were succeeding.

We experienced a couple of issues that made us think that being clearer on our values would be helpful.

Firstly, as the business grew, so did the headcount and we were having mixed success recruiting new staff. Some simply fitted in better than others and we became conscious that we were focusing too much on job skills in the process. Secondly, as Red Bull grew disproportionately to the beer brands, we also became aware that the culture of the Red Bull Company was very different to our own and this was having an impact.

With the help of our HR manager, we set out to be clearer on the values that made the business tick. We asked the people in the company to give their views on the things that made the business different and strong and we used this as the basis for our values blueprint.

This clarity of understanding helped us in a number of ways. It certainly improved the recruitment process helping us to focus on finding the right attitude and work ethic as well as job related skills. We conducted interviews in a more consistent way and the results of this meant we had more round pegs in round holes.

Perhaps more importantly, the process of defining these values seemed to create a sense of belonging amongst the people in the company. They too now had a better consciousness of what made the organisation tick.

Values	Behaviours
Keeping things simple	• Focus on what's important • Make decisions based on facts • Get on with it!
Brand driven	• Understanding the value of our brands • Understanding the needs of our brand owners and work hard to meet them • Uncompromising on brand values
Tenacity and Initiative	• Expect a lot from ourselves and others • Work hard to deliver results • Keep going when things get tough
People values	• Work together to achieve results • Respect each other and our differences • Put personal preferences aside to achieve team goals
Communicating and Influencing	• We listen (to customers, suppliers and each other) to work out what's needed • We use our influencing skills • We give and are open to constructive feedback
Commercial savvy	• Understand the difference between long-term goals and short-term tactics • Understand the importance of adding value to customers, brands and Ubevco • Getting the best deal we can
Customer service	• We only promise that which we can deliver • We listen to customers' needs and respond appropriately • We aim to exceed customer expectations

Often, lists of company values can look very similar and it is important to try and reflect the things that make you different. In our company, 'tenacity and initiative' were important values, and very much part of giving us the leading edge in the marketplace.

Simply put, our people worked hard but additionally there was a real drive that meant they were rarely beaten by problems either because they would not give up or because they used innovative thinking to find a solution.

Red Bull became one of the biggest brands in the on trade due to the Vodka Red Bull mix. Whilst this had been an easy sell into the leading-edge independent outlets, we had massive problems getting the major chains on board because of a pricing issue relating to the need to use only a half a can of Red Bull. The rigid pricing processes of the pub and bar chains made it harder for them to control the margin.

Our sales team kept going back to accounts to deal with the concerns but kept getting knocked back. They did not give up and came up with the concept of a 'perfect serve kit', which helped the bar achieve the right mix and, hence, protect against wastage. We knew that the bar staff did not really need this and probably would never used it but it convinced the bean counters at head office.

This solution came from within the team as their determination to succeed drove them to find the answer.

The list of values alone did not fully define the culture though. The culture was more complex and in many respects we still find it difficult to explain in full and set down in words.

Everyone in the organisation had a clear understanding of their role and their responsibilities. The business plan was shared with everyone and was clear on what each team needed to deliver. It became clear that some of the policies we had put in place were feeding the culture positively. For example, we had a bonus scheme based on the fundamental principle that everyone was rewarded irrespective of his or her role. If the company over achieved versus the objectives, a bonus pot was created from which everyone shared. This clearly helped develop the strong team ethos of working towards a common and shared goal.

Sometimes, there are inexplicable things that link people together and become part of the culture. These may include things that bare no relation to a person's job, or location or indeed level of seniority. If you like, they are things that put everyone on an equal footing and can develop to be something that is 'owned' as part of the organisation. We had a couple of these in Ubevco but perhaps the best example is football.

For some reason, there was a real love of football in the company and many people supported teams across the length and breadth of the UK and the divisions of the football league. It was something that people with little else in common would discuss, argue about and torment each other over. It even extended eventually to some of our brand owners and suppliers who gradually started to join in this everyday banter.

The 'Ubevco way' wasn't always all sweetness and light. It included a fierce drive to get things right and there were many occasions when it felt safer under the desk as the logistics manager had a frank exchange of views with the sales director; his sales performance having had been somewhat lacking versus forecast. But an hour later all would be forgotten over a drink in the pub.

Sometimes it felt like the office was filled with either people shouting at or laughing at or laughing with each other. Everyone had the right to an opinion but everyone also had the right to be treated respectfully; disagreements were quickly resolved. Whilst it is difficult to clearly define the culture, it is easy to say what it was and what it wasn't. It did include trust of each other to do the right thing, the right of the individual to say what they think, humour (often dark) and openness. It wasn't in any way political or bureaucratic.

At the end of the day, a shared vision held everything together. To those people that worked in the business for a long period, just the word Ubevco is enough to evoke deep feelings.

There are practical advantages having a cohesive culture that can be realised in various areas of the business:

- More consistent recruitment. You can ensure that you probe in interviews to ascertain not only job skills but also values.
- More effective control systems and reward systems. If your systems reflect your culture it will be much easier to get people to work with them and equally if your reward systems are also consistent with values then they are likely to be more motivating.
- More effective management of groups and teams within the organisation. As your business grows, the evolution of the culture will not rest just with you but with the managers that you develop. If they are embracing the culture, you can rest assured that it will be maintained.
- A way of bringing people together outside of their job specification.

Managing your culture externally

If understanding culture internally is difficult, then managing the external element can be even harder. As soon as you or a member of your company steps outside the door, there is a good chance that you will come across business cultures that are different to your own. If internally your company culture acts as the thing that brings people together, then in the outside world it acts as a way of expressing in part what your company is all about. It effectively helps to mould your reputation and will affect specifically things like views on your reliability and professionalism. If you are striving to achieve these values internally but they are not being consistently used in the outside world, you are not only missing an opportunity but arguably you could be undermining your business proposition. If you want to have a reputation for "fairness", you need to think about how you achieve that, not just inside the company but to the stakeholders outside of it.

It is not always easy for these values to be upheld when dealing with those outside of the business. In particular, when dealing with customers and suppliers, there is often the temptation to behave in line with their culture in order to endear yourself and importantly get the deal done. But this is a dangerous path.

The clearer you are about your culture internally, the easier this will be to manage it externally as you will recognise the things that affect it.

Ubevco worked with brands from all around the world that were owned by large organisations with very different cultures. Working with businesses from the Far East proved very different from businesses in the Americas and this brought new and interesting challenges.

The interesting thing about culture is that it touches everything – from the big questions about the sort of company you want to be to the daily trivia of who makes the coffee.

We worked with the Red Bull Company for six years and the cultures of the two businesses were different. They were different in a good way as we both had different jobs to do but there were differences that caused problems.

Red Bull had a strong view about the culture of the brand. The clarity of this vision was very much at the heart of the brand's success. Red Bull believed that 'living the brand' was important and, consequently, had an expectation that the people associated with it were also seen to be 'living the brand'.

For our sales people, in particular, there were many times when they had to switch from the Ubevco culture to the Red Bull one. For example, as the brand personality was about behaving unconventionally, Red Bull believed that the brand should not be sold to trade customers in a conventional fashion. In itself, this is fine and we didn't have an issue with it but it caused disconnect at times with the developing culture of the Ubevco business and this caused us some concern.

There were many examples of how this impacted the business but perhaps the best example is rooted in the trivial and in what on the surface seems like a very innocuous issue – wearing ties! Internally, we had a very relaxed management style. In and around the office there was a relaxed attitude to how people preferred to work and indeed dress. However, it was agreed by all, that a more professional stance was required in the outside world, hence, if we had visitors or were visiting customers or suppliers, we adopted a more formal approach and dress code.

As a result, our sales team dressed smartly when visiting customers as ultimately they were representing Ubevco. However, Red Bull decided that this was too traditional for its brand and insisted that our team dress informally when conducting Red Bull business. Ultimately, this wasn't too difficult to manage – we allowed the sales team to dress smartly without ties when on Red Bull business. The significance of this seemingly small issue hit home hard however when we next met with the senior Red Bull management from the parent company in Austria. Of all the business issues on the agenda for the brand (which at the time was showing year on year growth of 500%) the first thing they raised was their abhorrence that our sales team wore ties!

There may be occasions where you are dealing with very significant customers or suppliers where it is worthwhile thinking about their culture and how it could impact on your own and positively how you might work with it to encourage a better relationship between you. If you look for the areas of similarity, you may find advantages for your business relationship.

Over time we came to respect the different cultures of our stakeholders and appreciate that you can learn a lot from them.

- We learnt the importance of long-term relationships and the role for 'face' from our partnership with Asia Pacific Breweries in Singapore.
- We learnt to accept that Mexico ran on a different time clock to the UK, not just in terms of the time zone difference but also in respect to taking the time to make the right decision.

- We saw the ultimate passion for a brand working with South African Breweries where their management and employees display incredible degrees of loyalty to company and brand. (And the best party animals.)
- We learnt that Americans speak the same language as we do but in some respects are the most different culturally. We observed a very insular culture in terms of their willingness to work as a team and to consider and embrace outside views.
- Our relationship with Red Bull was often difficult as they displayed an unwillingness at times to take our advice on board. However, we came to realise that in the situation where they ultimately owned the brand then they had every right to the last word on the management of it.
- From many of our partners around the world we learnt a lot about making people feel welcome and the power of good hospitality.
- We came to understand that what may seem like a small cultural difference can, in fact be a much bigger deal in someone else's culture.

"A fish only discovers its need for water when it is no longer in it.
Our own culture is like water to a fish.
It sustains us."

Fons Trompenaars – author and consultant

The simple principles for a successful culture in a small organisation are:

- Don't underestimate the importance of culture – your own or that of another company.

- Take the time to think about it – what are the specifics of the culture you want? In the early days, this may not amount to more than a simple set of values but it will at least give guidance to the positives that you want to achieve.
- Make sure that you are consistent in how you communicate these values. Attaching to a website or to a mission statement is not enough. Through your actions, they need to be used on a daily basis to underpin and explain the decisions that are being taken in the business.
- Make sure that there is a "fit" between your culture and your corporate goals. Ubevco was aiming to be the best independent brand agency business in the UK, therefore, it was important that our people embraced the need to behave as brand builders.
- Lead by example. This is at the heart of developing your culture. If you have an aspiration to have a culture based on fairness, you have to play fair! You need to make sure that you "live the values" and can be seen by all to do so. You are the leader.
- Try to identify and capture things that are really personal to your organisation such as language, practices, habits and activities. Often this is the easiest way to bring your culture alive and make it understood within the organisation.
- Encourage everyone in the organisation to "live the culture", whether they are working with people inside or outside the organisation.

In summary

Creating the right environment gives you the opportunity to make going to work more enjoyable and improve the effectiveness of the organisation.

- Think about the physical environment and ensure that it works well first and foremost for you.
- Ensure that it creates a good impression to visitors.

- Try and ensure it meets the needs of other people that have to work in it.
- Think low cost – it is hard to justify how it adds to profit in the early days and there are more important calls on cash.
- The way you and your employees behave will influence your reputation so it is worthwhile thinking about how you can shape this to best effect.
- Your culture will help unify your organisation and is an easy way to influence new members of the organisation.

Chapter **14**

Staying on track

Once you have started trading and managed your way through the early chaotic days, eventually life will normalise. The day-to-day pattern of your business will become more regular and familiar and hopefully you will be able to start enjoying the fruits of your labour to date. You are in charge of your own enterprise, running things your way. Over the next few pages we are going to discuss the importance of keeping the plan on track.

Managing the business

As your business begins to establish itself, inevitably certain things will be different from how you planned them. These may relate to financial performance, operational facets or issues regarding personal and business relationships.

You can and should tinker with your plan; it is a working tool. Your original budget should always be maintained in place for the year but remember is it based on a set of assumptions which may or may not turn out to be true. It is important therefore that you regularly review the plan and revise it as your knowledge about the current situation develops.

A simple and very useful tool for any business is to report the results monthly with comparison to the original budget together with a rolling forecast of where your current financial year will end up.

Returning to the New Water Cooler business example we used in Chapter 6, a simple illustration of how you might build this kind of model is shown in the New Water Cooler Company Ltd Year 1 example.

TIPS

- Ensure that any additional processes that you use in the business to monitor performance – such as sales forecasts, production planning and delivery schedules – are able to dovetail into your overall plan. Keep it simple but ensure that all your data uses consistent formats.
- If you are not able to set up the systems yourself, get someone to do it for you.

Your financial plan is largely about numbers; are you producing the planned level of income and importantly are the cash flows behaving according to expectation? In many ways though, what is critical is the momentum rather than the absolute amount of the numbers achieved. If you are showing a good growth pattern, it doesn't really matter too much if you are running a couple of months behind schedule provided the trend is right. Any good bank manager will appreciate this point.

Managing expectation is very important to you, your colleagues/ partners and especially any financial backers.

You may make changes in your business model, such as pricing to your customers and lower or higher investment in employees or business infrastructure, to see what the impact on performance will be. However, try and avoid any panic reactions that send your business down a different strategic path. This applies equally whether you are doing better or worse than you expected.

There are many occasions where a new business has enjoyed some early success and started extending into other products or services that are not part of the core business idea. The way to grow is to extend the strategies (products/services) that are working for you in your business to a wider range of customers, and not to extend the strategies. It goes back to the point about playing to your strengths. Being small and flexible has many advantages but be careful that you do not exploit that flexibility by becoming reactive over strategic.

EXAMPLE | *Maintaining the focus*

The Red Bull organisation is a superb example of how to stay focused on your core product and extending its customer reach rather than get distracted by introducing related products, line or package extensions and changes. For probably at least a decade after it launched the product, Red Bull continued to produce only the now iconic 250 ml blue and silver can. There was no other size, no four or six pack, no low calorie version – just nothing else.

This was absolutely the right decision and helped everyone focus on maintaining the desired pricing and extending the

New Water Cooler Ltd Year 1

Rolling Forecast

Actual at June, Revised Forecast Jul–Dec

	Actual Results to Date						Rolling Forecast						Forecast	Original
	Jan	Feb	Mar	Apr	May	Jun	Jul	Aug	Sep	Oct	Nov	Dec	Total	Budget
Distribution & Rate of Sale														
-New Customers	8	12	10	9	13	20	25	8	10	8	6	5	134	120
-Total Customers	8	20	30	39	52	72	97	105	115	123	129	134		
-Refill Frequency per month	1	1	1	1	1.5	2	2.5	2	1.5	1	1	1		
-Bottles per order	2	2	2	2	2	2	2	2	2	2	2	2		
Sales Prices														
-Cooler Installation	£200	£200	£200	£200	£200	£150	£150	£200	£200	£200	£200	£200		
-Refill Bottles	£6	£6	£6	£6	£6	£6	£6	£6	£6	£6	£6	£6		
-Annual Clean (6 months)	£25	£25	£25	£25	£25	£25	£25	£25	£25	£25	£25	£25		
Sales Value														
-Cooler Installation	£1,600	£2,400	£2,000	£1,800	£2,600	£3,000	£3,750	£1,600	£2,000	£1,600	£1,200	£1,000	£24,550	£24,000
-Refill Bottles	£96	£240	£360	£468	£936	£1,728	£2,910	£2,520	£2,070	£1,476	£1,548	£1,608	£15,960	£12,360
-Annual Clean	£0	£0	£0	£0	£0	£0	£200	£300	£250	£225	£325	£500	£1,800	£1,500
	£1,696	**£2,640**	**£2,360**	**£2,268**	**£3,536**	**£4,728**	**£6,860**	**£4,420**	**£4,320**	**£3,301**	**£3,073**	**£3,108**	**£42,310**	**£37,860**

Variable Costs	**Unit Cost**														
Water Cooler	£35	£280	£420	£350	£315	£455	£700	£875	£280	£350	£280	£210	£175	£4,690	£4,200
Water Bottles	£2	£32	£80	£120	£156	£312	£576	£970	£840	£690	£492	£516	£536	£5,320	£4,120
Cleaning material A	£4	£0	£0	£0	£0	£0	£0	£40	£40	£40	£40	£40	£40	£240	£240
Cleaning material B	£2	£0	£0	£0	£0	£0	£0	£20	£20	£20	£20	£20	£20	£120	£120
Transport Cost	£5	£40	£100	£150	£195	£390	£720	£1,213	£1,050	£863	£615	£645	£670	£6,650	£5,150
Total Variable cost		**£352**	**£600**	**£620**	**£666**	**£1,157**	**£1,996**	**£3,118**	**£2,230**	**£1,963**	**£1,447**	**£1,431**	**£1,441**	**£17,020**	**£13,830**
Fixed Cost															
Office & Warehouse		£200	£200	£200	£200	£200	£200	£200	£200	£200	£200	£200	£200	£2,400	£2,400
Staff Costs		£1,250	£1,250	£1,250	£1,250	£1,250	£1,250	£1,250	£1,250	£1,250	£1,250	£1,250	£1,250	£15,000	£15,000
Admin & Marketing Costs		£550	£450	£250	£200	£400	£500	£350	£300	£300	£300	£250	£250	£4,100	£3,600
Total Fixed Cost		**£2,000**	**£1,900**	**£1,700**	**£1,650**	**£1,850**	**£1,950**	**£1,800**	**£1,750**	**£1,750**	**£1,750**	**£1,700**	**£1,700**	**£21,500**	**£21,000**
Total Costs		£2,352	£2,500	£2,320	£2,316	£3,007	£3,946	£4,918	£3,980	£3,713	£3,197	£3,131	£3,141	£38,520	£34,830
Profit/(Loss) By Month		**–£656**	**£140**	**–£40**	**£48**	**£529**	**£782**	**£1,943**	**£440**	**£608**	**£104**	**–£58**	**–£33**	**£3,790**	**£3,030**

Example continued

customer base by educating the public what the product was all about. There was also the very practical benefit of keeping the logistics simple as the brand extended its distribution into new markets.

Red Bull gradually introduced a four pack and six pack but it was many years before it introduced different sizes and types of can or bottle for its global markets. Moreover, it was well into the second decade of the product's life before it produced a diet version and a cola variant. At the time of writing, that remains the entirety of Red Bull's offering. There is no Red Bull chewing gum, no food bars, cologne or other product offshoots that some inferior brands try extending into. Red Bull's marketing and sponsorship programmes, on the other hand, have been extended globally and over a very wide range of sports, seeking always to convert potential consumers to its products. This is a great lesson on how to do things right.

Well that is all well and good you may say, because their business was producing great results. If the business is performing below expectation, you may need to consider whether your core proposition is flawed or needs some fundamental amendment. Just throwing additional products or services at your market to try and make up for an income shortfall is not the solution. It needs to be far more considered.

You will need to assess whether it is the basic idea that is the problem or the way the business is executing the proposition. Perhaps there is less volume in the market than you had anticipated. More likely, there will be aspects that just need some refinement to make things work. You should consider the following:

- pricing
- the way you are attracting your customers/clients
- the quality of your offering may need some improvement.

Identifying what needs tweaking can sometimes be difficult when you are embroiled in the day-to-day tasks. This is where a mentor can be helpful and seeking feedback from your customers and trade contacts too. It may be just small adjustments that can change your fortunes and give you that all important momentum.

Business performance is not just about the financial results though. This is the time to stand back and consider whether the whole experience of running your own business is living up to expectation. Remember, the aim was to provide you with a fulfilling job too. You should take the opportunity to review all aspects of your business structure to see if it can be improved. A little tinkering here and there can be very beneficial. This could involve getting extra help, maybe outsourcing a task or making some change to your environment or infrastructure arrangements.

In our own business life, one such 'tweak' had enormous benefits for us over a long period of time. We had originally located Ubevco near Tower Bridge believing that a London location was important from employee/customer/supplier perspective. After a year though, the mood started to change as life was becoming a little more predictable. Customers were bedded in and regular order patterns were forming. We had settled down the brand-owner relationships and discussions on the brands were shifting to reflect longer term planning. It was beginning to feel like we were going to be around for a while.

We realised at this point that as directors we were all travelling for 2–3 hours a day to the office. We all lived within 10 miles of each other in Surrey and doing almost the same journey.

And so, we made one of the best decisions of our Ubevco lives and agreed to relocate our offices closer to home. There was an element of selfishness here as fundamentally this suited the directors as opposed to our staff. It was an easy decision to justify on business grounds, as it effectively would put more of the directors' time into the business.

Having said all that, we did consider the impact on the staff before we made the decision. As with many companies, the location of head office has only a limited effect on the sales team given they spend much of their time in other places and if you are lucky sometimes even with customers.

The bigger concern was the office-based staff. Whilst we were few in numbers, we had a good team, working well and let's not forget had been very supportive through the setting up period. Only two of the team would be adversely affected by the move and we made arrangements to cover their extra costs and travel time.

We found a perfect office located in the centre of Dorking town, 10 minutes from the M25 motorway, 20 minutes from Gatwick Airport, 40 minutes from Heathrow Airport and with a mainline station to central London, and importantly, only about 10 minutes from our homes.

It looked good from all points. It was easy for the brand owners to get to from the airport, easy to get in and out of London, it wasn't too expensive and yet with a bit of work it would look impressive enough to those visitors we needed to impress. And there was a suitable selection of eating and drinking establishments on hand where we could go to make all those really important decisions.

We stayed there happily for over 10 years, expanding and contracting the office space over the years as the trials and tribulations of the business dictated.

The effect on our work-life balance was significant. It meant more time in the office, less time in the car and the comfort of being closer to home and children.

This example illustrates that you can and should make decisions that are for personal benefit and lifestyle enhancement as the business owner.

We have suggested that you keep the monitoring processes simple and focused, but this is not to say that you cannot employ other more sophisticated systems if you feel that is right for you and your business. Things like 360-degree feedback of management personnel, annual strategic review sessions, new product development or innovation initiatives may all have a place as part of an orchestrated review policy should you choose to introduce them. But, as we keep reinforcing throughout this book, do not lose sight of the simple principles upon which you started the business no matter how detailed and thorough some of your management tools become.

In Summary

As your business develops a more regular pattern, there are some simple principles to help ensure that the business stays on track to achieve your goals.

Firstly, by regular monitoring of your business plan you will know how the business is performing and keep abreast of the important financial issues. Use the business plan as a working tool, updating it regularly in line with actual performance data. This will also be very useful for you when communicating with important stakeholders such as the bank and investors.

Secondly, ensure that you focus on getting the core performance right. If you have given the time to deciding on your business idea you should not be distracted from it in the early days. If there are over or under-performance issues, make sure that you understand why and adjust accordingly. Do not be tempted to change strategic direction.

Thirdly, do not forget that this is your business. Make it work for you – the way you want it to be.

Chapter 15

Managing relationships

You may have noted that there is not a chapter in this book dedicated to human resource management. This is not because we do not recognise its importance. The reality of running a small business is it is unlikely that you will be able to think about HR as a distinct function for some time to come nor will be able to afford to hire someone to manage it for you. Some of the functions can be outsourced as we have indicated earlier but most of the day-to-day aspects will fall into your lap to manage. We feel it is more appropriate to think about them under the broader umbrella of relationship management, to include managing all human resource that you need to interact with, not just within your company.

In this chapter we will look separately at how you can best manage the relationships inside of your business with your partners, colleagues and employees where you have a great deal of influence and the often more complicated and difficult to manage relationships with your external suppliers, customers and stakeholders.

If we think about business in terms of just buying and selling, then we will only focus our time on how we can do more of both. It is easy to give relatively little thought to the impact that business relationships have on business success. In fact, the associations that we build are like the oil in our business engine. They smooth the operation.

But is there really a business benefit from creating good relationships? The simple answer is *yes*. The stress of dealing with difficult or acrimonious interactions can be significant and worth avoiding if at all possible. Like accounting for the cost of finding new consumers or customers, common sense dictates that it is more cost effective to have long-term relationships with colleagues, employees, suppliers, etc., than developing new ones. Long-term relationships bring stability whereas short-term ones tend to be more time consuming and costly. In this chapter, we will outline the basics of establishing good relationships, both inside and outside your business. We will also look at how to deal with the occasions when conflict occurs – it is not realistic to expect things to always be harmonious even if you manage them well.

Creating positive relationships

Investing time and effort in your business relationships will yield rewards.

In all areas of our life we have to manage relationships. We do it all the time – sometimes well and sometimes badly. It is probably the area of our lives that we think about least and yet has the greatest impact on our emotional health and happiness.

Creating positive relationships in a business sense is still about personal endeavour – you need to take responsibility for making it happen. A business relationship can range from formal, governed by a contract, to an indeterminable set of feelings (good and bad) about a person you do business with.

The definition of a 'good relationship' is difficult; it will differ according to the individual. However, we can all differentiate between positive affiliations where both parties are happy with each other and negative ones where they are not.

Some people have the natural aptitude for developing strong relationships; others have to work hard at it. This chapter therefore cannot give a definitive guide and there is not a one size fits all solution. You need to be personally reflective about the best way to achieve this given your own experience and personality.

Relationship management within your own company can be very different from the way you have observed in a large corporation. How we behave towards others – whether inside or outside the organisation – will usually reflect to some degree the culture of the organisation. So, you may well have experienced different styles, and it is worth reflecting on these to see where you have seen good relationship management. Use your actual experiences to guide you.

In line, therefore, with the thinking on the chapter about your business culture, the approach that you take needs to be in line with the value system that you adopt for your business. In fact, the way that you behave towards other people and organisations will provide a major lead to the people around you as to how they should behave.

Large companies have invested incredible sums in CRM (customer relationship management) programmes and business schools have generated vast tranches of research to the subject. Whilst both can have a bias in focus towards large companies, much of the work is also valid for smaller organisations and here are a few simple but relevant concepts that illustrate some of the thinking in the area.

Win/win relationships

If you have read Stephen Covey's (2004) *Seven Habits of Highly Effective People*, you will know about the concept of win/win relationships:

> *"Win/win is a frame of mind and heart that constantly seeks mutual benefit in all human interactions. Win/win means that agreements or solutions are mutually beneficial, mutually satisfying. With a win/win solution, all parties feel good about the decision and feel committed to the plan. Win/win sees life as a cooperative, not a competitive arena. Win/win is based on the paradigm that there is plenty for everyone, that one person's success is not achieved at the expense or exclusion of the success of others."*

It is as simple as it sounds – both parties have to benefit in order for the relationship to be healthy long term. Covey cleverly uses examples in both a personal and business context thus allowing us to see how we can live both sides of our lives in cooperation. He identifies other types of relationships, including the win/lose relationship which we are much more familiar with in the business world. For sure, at times this is appropriate. But for those relationships that we have identified as important to us/our business in the long term, the win/win model is far more productive but requires an attitudinal shift.

Emotional intelligence

If you have been involved in recruitment in recent years, you will probably be familiar with the concept. It suggests that IQ is too narrow a measure of an individual's leadership ability. EI aims to identify the interpersonal skills that are needed by today's leaders. In simple terms, EI is the ability to inspire, influence and develop others whilst managing conflict. In other words, it is about managing the myriad of relationships we have in our business dealings. Within a small business you may be solely responsible for doing this. It is about the ability to understand firstly self and then others and their feelings.

Face

Eastern culture is different from western culture in many ways. In a business sense, the way they conduct relationships is fundamentally different to ours. We would add the caveat here that this applies to the way businesses from an eastern culture relate to each other and also that "face" differs between cultures in the east. In the Western economy we tend to understand the term "face" as relating to pride. In fact, it is something different; face is the basis of a value system founded on the benefit to the group, rather than a value system founded on the individual, as in the West. The interesting aspect of face is that it promotes harmonious relationships based on respect, trust, patience and longevity.

The physical differences are massive. In Eastern business relationships the existence of negotiation is minimal compared to that in Western society. It is relatively unnecessary as there is an understanding that both parties will do the right thing to promote the harmonious relationship.

We are not suggesting that this is a principle that can be readily adopted but it can contribute to our understanding of what can underpin good long-term relationships.

Key points

These concepts about relationships suggest you should focus on making them:

- productive
- long term
- involve trust, honesty and openness
- proactively managed.

Steps involved in creating positive relationships

Managing relationships effectively implies some degree of process.

1 The first step is to accept your share of responsibility for the health of the relationship. That is not to say that,

ultimately, you can dictate your terms to create a positive association. As we will discuss later, sometimes the other party will not define the relationship in the same way that you do.

2. Identify which are the most important to your business; this will guide where you invest your time.
3. In addition, identify those which will be beneficial in the long term. It is not always true that all relationships should be long term. You may find some benefit in changing supplier in some situations.
4. The next stage of the process is to think about where the power in any relationship lies. If you are a customer, you probably have more power. As an employer, you have the greater power. As a supplier, you probably are the weaker party when it comes to negotiating terms. A balanced relationship relegates the use of power.
5. You need to think about what you would like to gain from this relationship in the long term and what you think the other party would wish to gain. This should allow you to see the points of mutual interest/benefit and the points where the parties will disagree.

Internal relationships

Whether you are working with a number of partners in a consultancy/agency business or you have employees, the principles are the same. Importantly, with your internal colleagues you share the same business goals and this will underpin your relationship. You are looking to get the best from your colleagues or employees as a means of motivating them towards your shared goals.

Most people want the same things from their work:

- money – fair recompense for their efforts
- job satisfaction – to enjoy their work
- opportunity to develop – this does not necessarily apply to all (some people just want to do what they do) but most wish to see a future where they have the opportunity to get more of the previous two points

- to be treated well – justly as a minimum, fairly if possible and ideally to be valued as someone who contributes meaningfully for what they do.

So, if you provide all this as part of an associate's work experience, what should you expect to achieve in return?

- Hard work
- Loyalty
- Commitment to the business objectives
- Harmony within the company.

On paper, it looks easy but the reality is slightly different. The point about a relationship is that it is a living thing. You cannot just put things in position and expect nothing to change. The onus is on you as the leader of the business to illustrate your commitment to maintaining good relationships with those you work with. In the context of your own business, think about how you can facilitate the positive feelings that you wish to nurture.

Recruitment

The beginning of your relationship with employees is self evidently when you recruit them.

Recruitment is complicated; the requirements of your recruitment process will depend upon the needs of your specific business and the nature of the person you are looking to hire. Recruiting a sales manager will be very different from trying to hire 100 temporary employees for a particular task. The size of your business and the number of employees in it will influence how sophisticated you need to be in your approach. This is a very developed function and as we discussed in Chapter 7 you could elect to outsource to a specialist agency.

There are several books that can help you specifically on this subject, a few of which are listed at the end of this book. Any large bookstore will have a selection in the business section. Similarly, there are various websites that offer general guidance:

www.acas.org.uk
www.businesslink.gov.uk
www.employmentdocumentcompany.co.uk

As with all the major functions of your business, the key is to spend a little time thinking about what you are trying to achieve when you are recruiting and creating a plan to achieve it. This applies irrespective of how many people you employ. The most important thing is that you find the very best candidates for whatever tasks you need completing. If you plan to employ a large number of employees you will benefit from using a consistent approach with a number of ready-made tools such as job descriptions, employment contracts, employee handbooks, etc.

The benefits of using a recruitment agency primarily sit in the "time-saving" category. They can organise any advertising for the role, create advertisements, screen applications, conduct first round interviews, run candidate assessments and profiling, etc. If you have a large number of employees or you are seeking high-profile senior managers, this may be a useful option. However, all of the above comes at a not insignificant cost and in most circumstances you can do it yourself.

The benefits of running your own recruitment are significant. When you interview candidates you have an early opportunity to promote your business and no one will do this as well as you. If you want the best candidates in your company, you will be competing for them. Even in times of economic downturn, the better candidates will find work.

The key to really successful recruitment is when you find the perfect balance of the right job skills for the role and the right personality fit for your business. Therefore, as discussed in Chapter 13, understanding the values you are looking for will increase the success rate of your recruitment. You can develop interview questions that do not merely test candidates' job skills but explore how they will fit alongside the rest of the company. Especially in a small business, this is very important. The need to simply get along is more important in a small team but there is an opportunity to drive your business with people who support your business values. This is a harder brief for a recruitment agency to fulfil.

The physical mechanics of the process will take up some of your time but if you get organised it is usually manageable. There are plenty of proforma tools to help you with things like contracts of employment and job descriptions. These do not need to be overly complicated as long as they cover the key criteria that are important to your business.

If you feel that you need to advertise to attract applications, the most important thing is to advertise it in the best possible place – think targeted selection rather than every publication possible. Advertising space is expensive and therefore avoid as much as you can.

Good sources of potential employees are often more direct:

- current employees can often recommend others
- customers may be aware of good candidates in other businesses
- local schools, colleges and universities
- Job Centre Plus
- your network of current and past colleagues
- your own website.

Managing your internal relationships

In our experience, there are some easy ways that enable you to demonstrate your commitment to your internal colleagues.

1 Remuneration

Have a clear policy on remuneration including when it will be reviewed. This does not have to be a complicated policy but it needs to be clear and you need to apply it very consistently. If you make exceptions for individuals it will undermine the policy.

> In Ubevco, we reviewed salaries each year. The salary review normally consisted of two elements: a general pay rise based on inflation and a performance review based on the nature of an individual's job performance. In a small company it is unlikely that structure will be very rigid. We found that we needed to change the nature of individual's jobs regularly to meet the changes in the business. These processes allowed us to reflect where someone had taken on more responsibility over recent months.

Sometimes it is not possible to pay people as much as they would like – often people feel they are worth more than you do and sometimes you simply cannot afford to do so. But by being clear and consistent on remuneration you avoid the situation where individuals feel hard done by.

> When we started the company, we had five shareholders – three managing partners and two sleeping partners. We put in place a very simple but effective shareholders agreement that clearly stipulated how both the executives would be remunerated and how we would deal with profit and dividend allocation. This can be particularly important if you need to retain profits within the business for financial stability.

If you cannot afford high salaries, there are other ways to reward people.

2 Performance management

Most effective businesses have systems that allow them to review the performance of the employees. Again, this can be as simple or sophisticated as you think necessary for your business. Remember, it is your business and you are likely to have to do it. It is another area where consistency is really important if people are to feel they are being managed fairly.

There are many advantages to using performance management:

- It allows you to build and improve the performance of your business – it can have a significant financial benefit.
- It allows you to demonstrate that you are prepared to invest in the individuals within the company and develop them in line with their long-term goals.
- It provides an important way of managing any employees that are not performing in line with the business requirements.
- It can allow your employees a platform to feedback to you on your performance as a manager.

3 Incentives

Bonuses are a way of showing your commitment to those around you by volunteering to share the financial gains. You will get most benefit if this is established early and so it works both as an incentive to achievement as well as an additional financial reward.

> We used bonuses extensively in the business. As a young company, it allowed us to pay modest salaries to everyone in the company (directors included) on the understanding that if we reached our targets then we would share any additional margin with everyone (irrespective of their job). It was a very simple scheme – for every case of drinks we sold over our target, 50% of the margin earned would go into a margin pot which would then be divided out based on a % of salary – e.g. everyone might earn an extra 10% of their salary. In the year that we saw Red Bull suddenly accelerate in growth, everyone in the business earned an extra six months' salary as bonus. This became legend within the business and had a very positive impact for many more lean years to come. It meant that we hadn't had to increase salaries long term but had rewarded people fairly when we could.

The important thing about bonuses is they should be achievable if they are to be motivational. You need to be very clear on the criteria and be careful that you don't engender jealousy if some members of your organisation are excluded. It can be an area fraught with problems but in our experience if managed carefully can be a very effective way of showing your commitment to your people whilst being financially sensible. A clear and simple scheme was always the most effective.

We firmly believed in the team ethic, that everyone benefited equally from the bonus scheme irrespective of individual roles or performance. We were still able to reward exceptional individuals through promoting them or by salary review. The benefit we saw from everyone pulling together for the same-shared bonus was a significant factor in our success and culture.

4 Holiday policy

Holidays are very important to people. They are highly valued. Whilst you are legally obliged to give holidays if you behave in such a way as to only ever give the statutory minimum you are ignoring the importance of this benefit to the individual and potentially missing out on a way to reward people for relatively little cost. Again, it is helpful if you have a clear policy on both how holidays are allocated and the process that enables people to take them. Whatever your policy on holiday, you should be honourable in the way you behave when people wish to take their holidays. There is nothing worse than an employer who is begrudging when a colleague takes his or her well-earned holiday.

In Ubevco, we used holidays as a financial reward in a number of ways. Firstly, for everyone who had worked in the business for five years we gave them an additional day's holiday for every year that they worked. Everyone in the business was entitled to this and it proved to be a very envied perk by the newer members of the company. The cost to the business was low relative to the value both to the individual and loyalty to the company. Secondly, we had a year where we made virtually no profit and we were not able to increase salaries. Instead we gave everyone an additional three days' holiday. This did not affect the P & L and yet maintained the morale of the people in the business. It allowed them to take on board bad news and at the same time they felt that we were doing our best for them. Win/win.

5 Bringing people together

This is a very good way of encouraging strong relationships both between yourself and your colleagues and also between colleague and colleague. It can be especially important if you have different teams within your business as it allows you to manage relationships across the team network.

We became big fans of bringing people together because the benefits were so obviously clear. Whenever we launched a new

product we had a company conference. If we didn't have a launch then we would find another opportunity in the year – maybe Christmas for example to get together. On the face of things, this would be a cost to the business but we always took the opportunity of having a business element to the event before perhaps the more important bit – the opportunity to socialise.

Outside of big events, we always encouraged people to get together as a means of building strong face-to-face relationships in addition to the virtual and telephone contact they had day to day.

6 Respect

Critical to your relationship with those around you is respect. You need to have their respect before you will gain their trust. Respect will come from a number of areas. You need to be seen as honest, fair and leading them in the right direction. They will look at your behaviour and follow your lead. So if you want them to work hard, they need to see you doing the same. Also it is critical that respect is a two way street. If individuals do not feel respected, they will quickly disengage from the relationship.

7 Communication

In today's virtual world an increasing amount of communication takes place via indirect medium such as email and text. In large organisations it may be difficult to engage in face-to-face communication and indeed even in a small company it is not always possible or efficient to do so. Whilst these types of communication bring certain advantages, the limitations are also well documented.

The relatively small scale of your organisation will allow you to manage the way you communicate with your colleagues. The best way to communicate, especially on important matters, is face to face. Resist the temptation to deliver difficult messages via email when you can do it face to face. And encourage others to behave the same. At the very least, this will reduce misunderstanding associated with email and messaging.

Create an environment where everyone finds it easy to raise issues and concerns. You will find that problems are highlighted faster, which allows you to react more quickly.

8 Discipline and grievance policy

This is an important way of clearly communicating your expectations of general behaviour and the consequences of contravening them. The policy should be a two way street and offer the employees the opportunity to raise grievances too. This area is a difficult one and you would be advised to ensure that your policy is legally sound. The importance of this policy is to avoid situations where you later encounter employment tribunals. You need to have a clear and appropriate disciplinary process that you follow carefully. Again, there are many sources of detailed advice available on the internet:

www.cipd.co.uk
www.acas.org.uk

The key to strong internal relationships is to do your bit to ensure that those around you feel motivated, fairly remunerated, valued and respected. Putting in place the policies to ensure fairness is, we suggest, the minimum that you do. Ultimately, it will be your everyday actions that influence your relationships. Having good relationships with employees does not mean that you always have to be the nice guy. There will always be situations where you need to do something that will be unpopular. Importantly, if you are seen as a reasonable and fair manager, your actions are much more likely to be accepted.

External relationships

Whilst internally you will share goals with your colleagues, with your external relationships you are likely to have different agendas. You need to identify the key external relationships for your business and try to understand their objectives. This allows you to keep focused on the important things. There are two extra things you can do.

1 Try to identify the areas where you have a mutual shared interest. These are less likely to be the same financial goals but they can still be very important as a means of solidifying the relationship. You need to demonstrate that you understand what is important to the other party. This will at the very least keep the relationship stable and more than likely also engender respect and trust.

2 Be reliable and deliver what you commit to. This is important in every relationship but especially important in those that are less directly within your control. If you promise to do something, large or small, make sure you do. This is such a simple way of proving that you are reliable. If for some reason you cannot deliver, you must come clean as soon as you can. The worst situation is where the other party has an expectation that is not delivered and they are surprised by it. Reputations are easily lost in such circumstances as word soon spreads within organisations and externally within your particular industry. Your failure to deliver may soon have a knock-on effect which can be a cause of great distress.

Our brand owners were our most important relationships. Without their brands we didn't have a business. In the UK, it is difficult for international brands to earn profit due to high duties. It was important therefore that this was not the only criterion used to assess our performance. We needed to focus on other objectives to build these relationships. The management of the brands, both in terms of the strategic plans we developed and the execution of these plans in the market was very important to all the brand owners – it is the job they do themselves in their home market. We needed to prove to them that we did that job well. This built their faith that they had the best distributor in the UK and kept their investment in place.

Sometimes too, your personal non-business related behaviour can create a bond that positively influences the business relationship. We held one Ubevco conference in the Czech Republic, home of the Pilsner Urquell brand that we represented. After a trip around their magnificent old brewery in Plzen, we organised a game of football against

the brewery team. In the clubhouse afterwards, Dennis was persuaded to perform his party trick of drinking a pint of beer standing on his head. The brewery team found this hilarious and Dennis became somewhat of a local legend. Many times thereafter when we needed urgent help with supply or materials we got preferential treatment because of 'that mad Englishman who stood on his head!'

Key points

- Good relationships are better than bad ones – physically, emotionally and financially.
- Strong relationships with colleagues and employees will improve motivation and performance.
- Focus attention on the areas of mutual interest.
- Be consistent in your behaviour.
- Relationships always need to be balanced – the long term will involve give and take.

Managing conflict: must win or compromise?

Even in the best of relationships you cannot hope to agree all the time and difference of opinions will always occur. The question is how to steer your way through periods of conflict to a position of resolution and maintenance of the good relationship.

We have already touched on the balance of power in a relationship. Often, this power ratio is most important when there is disagreement. We are usually most sensitive to this when we are on the wrong side of the power balance and feel that we are being pressured to do something. As a small company, this may be a regular thing with your external associations. You also need to be conscious that with your internal relationships you will be the stronger party and be careful how you use the power card.

The issue is not about whether you can agree to disagree; it is about how you go about agreeing to disagree.

Pick your battles

You need to be realistic about what you can expect when you have a position of conflict. You cannot hope to win all your battles and so what is important is that you win the most important ones.

We often joked that life would be wonderful if we didn't have customers, brand owners or employees to create problems. In reality, business life is full of differences of opinion. The argument is often won not by the best thought-out position but the party with most power. This can lead to a great deal of frustration if you are a small business.

Given the type of business we were in, we were especially susceptible to this. Of course, we had all the usual irritating disagreements with suppliers and employees (the unsolvable perfect car policy for example). In addition, though, we had unusually complex relationships to manage in the form of our brand principals. In theory, they had the most power as they could take the brands away. We had contracts with these companies but at the end of the day if they did not want to work with you any longer, they could find a way out.

Success in these relationships on the surface relied on business performance. As long as we were delivering our targets then we were on fairly safe ground. Yet, we were involved with the management teams of these companies for 52 weeks a year and if there was not a good day-to-day working rapport life would get difficult very quickly.

The quality of the working relationships varied enormously and the point is that there will always be differences. Sometimes they are caused by personality, sometimes by culture and sometimes by competency. Always assuming you are right and the other party is wrong however simply will not solve anything.

You need to be able to identify where a conflict threatens your position significantly and/or strategically.

> *We experienced a problem where a potential new brand wanted us to share the exclusive distribution rights with another sales operation. We believed this could undermine our ability to manage pricing effectively on the brand and more importantly could threaten our overall strategy*

for exclusivity across our portfolio. We knew this was a battle we had to win and if we could not win the argument then we would walk away from the deal. In the end, the brand owner agreed to our full exclusivity.

In a different situation, one of our brand owners wanted to invest a significant proportion of the marketing budget on a sponsorship deal, which we believed would have little direct effect on sales. There were benefits from this sponsorship back in the brand owner's domestic market. We backed down, therefore, on the basis that the brand owner had more to gain and lose. We agreed we would monitor the effect in our market to determine future plans.

The difference between these examples is simple. The first situation was a "must win" as it would potentially affect our strategic position. In the second situation, the maintenance of the relationship in the long term was more important than winning this particular argument.

Finally, winning is all well and good but the bigger emphasis should always be on maintaining the health of the relationship. So, gloating is never helpful! If you are clear on which battles you must win, you can also manage better the battles which you are prepared to lose and, hopefully, still achieve a position of some compromise.

Compromise and the path of least resistance

The best solution is always when the other party thinks it has got what it wants and so sometimes the cleverest debate convinces the other party that they want the same as you! There will be many occasions that are not a "must win" and in these situations the ideal is to gain a position of compromise rather than to just concede completely.

Rather than think about it as just a negotiation, the path of least resistance looks for the smoothest solution. By focusing on the needs of the other party you can try to steer the path that is closest to delivering what you want whilst giving the other party what they want. This might sound obvious but usually in negotiation we focus on what we want and the degree to which we can afford to give ground.

The most important thing is to ensure that you steer a path that moves the issue forward giving both parties some benefits. If you can do this and not have to give up all the concessions on your part, you will have found the path of least resistance.

This is a very healthy position. It means you have remained in charge of finding the solution and whilst you may have to relinquish some points you are guiding the solution.

Guidelines

- It is important that you understand the needs of the other party. Often disagreements can involve complex situations. It is critical to have understanding if you are to be able to plot the path of least resistance.
- Therefore, you will need to try and stand back and gain deeper understanding. Often arguments do not seem to make sense, which can be an indication that you are missing something. You may feel that you have proposed a very good plan or solution, which is being refused. Maybe the conflict is not directly related to your plan. You need to improve your understanding to get beneath the skin of the issue.
- This may require you to listen more carefully – a skill we often do not utilise enough.
- If you probe more fully and explore other issues around the subject, you may unearth deeper issues.
- If all else fails, be direct and say that you don't see the issue.

> On one occasion, APB was arguing that our margin was too high. We did not want to concede on this as it had a major profit implication long term.
>
> When we probed more deeply, it turned out that APB wanted to find some money to invest in the Chinese restaurant sector.

> Once we understood this, we were able to propose that we would add additional sales resource into the sector. They were happy with this plan. We retained our margin and though we had to invest money in extra sales resource we would generate extra business as a result.
>
> Win/win!

It is easy to see how the principles of "face" adopted by Eastern cultures lead to naturally long-term relationships – the onus is on the other party to do the right thing for the relationship as opposed to themselves. It is unlikely that this is practical in Western culture but the basic principle of wanting the other party to be satisfied is a good one.

Key points

- Where conflict occurs, be clear on your goals – is it a battle you must win or can you afford to compromise.
- Your behaviour will then be guided by this goal.
- In situations where you need to compromise, the best result will be gained if you fully understand the needs of the other party. This allows you to see the best solution for you.
- If you fail to resolve the conflict, try to at least keep the relationship alive so you are in a position to rebuild in the future.
- Take responsibility for managing conflict as it will bring you the best solution.

In summary

Investing time and effort in building strong and effective business relationships is important to both the physical and emotional aspects of your business.

- There is usually a financial benefit to strong long-term associations.

- They contribute to a positive business culture.
- You will feel like you share goals, even when you may also have exclusive goals as well. There needs to be an area of mutual benefit.
- You will have a lot of influence on the relationships you have within the company and this gives you the chance to positively motivate the people you work with.
- The external relationships you have are harder to control but you can still influence most negotiations. Look for your positions of power.
- To manage conflict well, you need to apply the same principles of managing good relationships. You need to understand what is important to the other party and try to deliver as much as you can whilst achieving what you need.

Chapter 16

Managing growth

In the first year or so of your business, most of your efforts will be focused on making your relatively small company efficient, dynamic and most importantly profitable. If your plan is working, the next challenge is to manage growth.

There are three areas that you will need to consider:

- the financial issues surrounding cash flow
- the impact on the infrastructure
- the potential affects on the culture of the organisation.

There is an assumption in most of the business world that you must strive for growth at all cost. Certainly some is essential to ensure that your business can generate sufficient income for you to maintain its real value. However, it may not be your first priority. You may have "lifestyle" goals, which include motivation to manage your own family income with a more balanced way of life. In which case, driving for growth may be less of an issue.

Where it is highly attractive, is for those business owners who seek increasing financial rewards and potentially a lucrative exit some years down the line. If this is the case, your three-year plan probably reflects some growth objective to both your income and profitability.

Financial issues

Usually the most critical concern about growth is how to fund it. Bankers seem almost as obsessed with "overtrading" as they are about their bonus culture. Overtrading is generally defined as a situation in which a business is growing its sales faster than it can finance them. It is associated with unmanageable increases in the level of amounts due from customers and owed to suppliers which in turn compound overall liquidity. This concern ought to be easily addressed provided that the business is growing profitably not eroding margins and by applying sufficient resource to ensure that debts are still collected promptly and securely.

If you have already outsourced your debt collection, this will be helpful, as almost by definition they have the ability to handle more of the specific task they are performing for your business. You can also choose a second outsource company for that specific task if the situation justifies it.

At Ubevco, we experienced quite exceptional increases in turnover within just a few years of formation. We were delighted to achieve sales of £6.7m and make a profit in our first calendar year, but this level of trade was soon to become a distant memory. Led by Red Bull but with strong growth across the whole of our drinks portfolio, we quadrupled turnover in just two years to £23m and we then almost quadrupled it again the next year with £90m of sales.

The arrangements we had made when setting up Ubevco came into their own. Red Bull were happy to continue with a consignment stock arrangement whereby they retained the legal ownership of the stock until the point that Ubevco sold it, we would pay them each week for the previous week's sales. This gave them a good quick cash flow and we were always able to pay them because through our factoring arrangement we were always able to borrow, if we needed to, an amount equal to 80% of what we sold the previous week. Included in the value of what we sold was VAT and our own margin. We would always have enough money to pay our bills, as long as the factor company were able to grow with us, and as the sales were profitable they amply covered any extra interest and factoring costs we had to pay.

To put the levels of funding in context, at the end of our first year of trading we were borrowing amounts in the region of £200,000 but just four years later these levels needed to be as high as £10 m. If we had financed the business any other way, we would have had to renegotiate countless times with heavy banking fees and risk a weaker negotiating position rather than a stronger one as we grew.

But for our factor company, growing with us was an absolute no brainer. Our customer base of around 400 invoicing points did not change significantly as the sales exploded, the number of orders did increase but most of the growth was in simply bigger orders. Moreover, most of our customers were credit-worthy, nationally known names and so the quality of the debtor book was generally first class. We were as good a piece of business as any factor company could wish for.

Now that it's not to say that every business can mirror the circumstances that we were able to enjoy, but the roots of our solution lay in our original decision to involve the key suppliers in our funding chain. If you address such issues ahead of time and are appreciative of each other's problems and concerns, you can often find a creative solution that helps all parties deal with the financing.

If you already have growth planned into your long-term plan, you need to think about how you will manage the funding and especially the cash flow.

Growing the infrastructure

Availability of finance is not the only part of your operation that comes under strain as you grow.

- Can you physically supply the extra quantities of your product or service that your business is providing?
- Will you be able to adequately deliver to your customers?
- Will you need more employees to deliver the extra business?

You need to be considering in advance if there any constraints to these supply issues and you need to factor in the increased costs to the business, especially if the costs are fixed in nature. If there are limitations on how quickly you can grow, you need to manage this. Letting customers down by a failure to supply can soon ensure that your rapid business growth turns into rapid decline. As far as solutions are concerned, once again good planning and problem sharing with your suppliers and business partners is the key.

The benefit of outsourcing again shines through in growth situations as much of the increase can be absorbed by your existing outsourcers or by adding additional ones.

> As we have already discussed, all the Ubevco product storage and delivery was outsourced.
>
> The strategy served us well logistically especially when we started to grow quickly, through the use of good quality business partners. That is not to say that things stood

still and we changed some of the companies we used a few times to help improve costs and service efficiency.

When the growth of Red Bull began to accelerate, we needed to make a major change to the logistics model. The initiative involved moving to a rail solution, which helped both the Red Bull company and us reduce costs, by moving to a rail-linked warehouse in Daventry. It was a sight to behold as the weekly train from Austria carrying nothing but silver and blue cans pulled alongside the warehouse to be unloaded directly by forklift truck and readied for its return journey. It just went back and forth through the channel tunnel from Daventry to the Austrian factory – the only pity being that it usually went back empty.

The fact that this function was outsourced gave us the flexibility to initiate this change.

During the early years of your business there is much merit in retaining as much flexibility to your cost structures as possible. This will enable you to grow when you need to or indeed to constrict if the business environment hardens for any reason. The benefit of long-term business relationships in this situation are invaluable. You need to work with companies who will work with you during good times and bad.

The impact on the internal operation

Many of the individual tasks within your business may cope with the expansion more easily than you might imagine. You will find that the boost in morale from seeing some growth in the company will make the need to work a bit harder for all concerned easier to swallow.

In many ways, the hardest areas to manage will be at the very core of what you do; the strengths that you focused on when you started and designed your core proposition. With growth, it is likely that you will need to add resource to help you with the core tasks. It does not matter whether you are a very small business, with a handful of people, or a larger organisation, to be able to add such resource whilst maintaining the skills, style and culture you have established is one of the hardest parts of managing growth. We certainly found that to be the case.

As 1999 progressed, the Red Bull brand moved through that important point on the life cycle curve where consumer pull kicks in. As the rate of sale in current distribution increased, it became increasingly easy to bring on new distribution. By the end of that year, sales of Red Bull were up five fold on the previous year. A new set of challenges faced the business as Red Bull had changed from being one of six products in our portfolio to accounting for over 80% of the volume.

You would have thought that the relationships between our company and all our brand owners would have been exceptional. Sadly, that was not the case. Despite the strong growth on their brands the beer brand owners were increasingly nervous about the performance of Red Bull and its impact on the dynamics in the company. They were concerned that their brand would get reduced focus going forward. There seemed simply to be no pleasing the Red Bull Company either, but at least all our employees were happy. They had all earned six months' salary as a bonus for their performance.

The issue related to our core philosophy. We set out to offer a small number of brands with a focused sales resource. The beer brands were worried that they would no longer get this, and Red Bull was concerned partly that it wouldn't get enough resource, and partly that the resource in place didn't reflect the company's values. So Red Bull wanted more people and a different culture. The culture of the Ubevco team had been instrumental in achieving the success so far and so this was a difficult dilemma.

Managing the turnover from £6m to £106m financially and logistically had been relatively comfortable but the pressure from Red Bull to add people was less manageable.

A compromise was reached and we agreed to introduce a specialist soft drinks team starting in January 2000 of around 70 people and in return they improved our contractual term.

However, managing this part of the growth was by far the most difficult issue we faced.

We suddenly had to move in directions that were culturally at odds with the Ubevco way. We could no longer as a management team keep everything very tight with a small and trusted senior team. There was inter-company rivalry regarding soft drinks versus beer people and, yes, the dreaded company politics began to creep in. Then, of course, there was the considerable management effort in the actual process of interviewing and hiring so many people in a short space of time. A recruitment agent was retained to help the process and suddenly we were into running assessment centres and personality tests – not to mention spending close to £400,000 on their fees.

So by mid 2000, we had a fully manned staff of around 130 people, all of whom of course needed paying and most needed a company car, phones, home computer and managing. This part of the growth was too fast and too costly. The distraction lost us sales rather than added sales and the extra costs were straight off the bottom line which is painful to recall, even though the company remained profitable.

Whilst we believed in outsourcing many key functions, the lesson we learned is that when it comes to the people who are going to work in your business, you need to retain control and manage as much as you can yourself. It had been an unrealistic expectation that we could successfully grow and restructure the number of employees at the rate we agreed to with Red Bull and it not only cost us lots of potential profit, it nearly lost us the true Ubevco spirit that we knew and loved.

Of course, in this situation the growth levels were unusually high. However, we believe that the type of problems we wrestled with over culture maintenance, expectation management and human resource issues are common ones that will occur at some stage in a business' life.

As the owner though you are always able to make a choice and if you prefer to slow down growth to maintain other important facets of your business then you can. Equally, you can go with it and accept that cultural change may happen, even management and ownership change in the fullness of time.

These choices may be linked to your longer-term goals for the business. Some change is inevitable as your business develops and we will discuss this in more detail in the next chapter.

In summary

Growth is a good thing. There is a big condition though – as long as you stay in control of it. It may well be that the customer demand for whatever you are selling is greater than you expected. You cannot necessarily control this. But you need to stay in control of your business.

- Plan for the eventuality that your business will grow.
- Understand the financial impact and work out what options are available to you to fund the growth.
- If growth requires you to extend your operations in some way, try to build in as much flexibility as you can until such time that you have more certainty around the long-term position.
- Take great care not to lose the core essence of what makes your company tick. It is the successes of the past that are creating the potential for greater success in the future. So try not to throw the baby out with the bath water!

Chapter 17

Embracing change

So far we have looked at the key aspects of setting up your business and putting it on the right track for success through strong strategy and planning. But nothing in this world stays the same for long. It really does not matter whether you are a small business or a large conglomerate, every business will face obstacles and opportunities that will require it to change and adapt over time. By this, we do not mean small tactical changes to your plan; we are talking about the need to deal with something that has a significant impact.

Managing change is probably the most talked about, consulted on, researched area of business today. Change, we are told, is inevitable in a world where the speed of development of new and improved products and services is clearly escalating and the natural life cycle shortening. Change can come with both positive and negative implications for your company.

We experienced a particularly severe change project after five years of trading which threatened our business and we will use this example to illustrate the key points.

It began on a sunny afternoon in July 2001. Our business was turning over £105 million per year and we employed 130 people in the organisation. We were in a meeting with the managing director of Red Bull UK and he began the meeting with the following...

We think that you guys have done an amazing job, but...

The word 'but' is usually followed by something negative. In our case, it was the news that Red Bull believed the time was right to take the sales of the brand back in house and do it themselves. It launched us on a major period of change.

By December, we had to remove £90 million from our turnover projections and say goodbye to 70 of our staff. However, we had found our way through a process which allowed us to reorganise our business making it better suited to the current market in which we were operating and most importantly reinvigorate our enthusiasm for what we were doing.

Understanding the dynamics of change

Change affects all aspects of our lives but for most people it creates feelings of uncertainty and sometimes fear. The sense of discomfort comes from the relative lack of clarity that the future holds versus the status quo even when the status quo may be problematic. For many these feelings generate a reluctance to change; a preference to hold on to a less than perfect status quo. Sometimes, however, especially in our business lives, we are unable to resist change and are forced towards a more uncomfortable and vague position.

Change, ultimately, is a journey and whilst this involves physically altering aspects of our business it also includes managing those feelings of fear and trepidation that seem to sit along side it. The journey takes us from the present to a new status quo. The question is how to get between the two with a best fit for your company and with the least challenge to your emotional state.

Triggers for change

Effectively there are only two triggers:

- *Reactive change*: this is imposed upon you by issues either inside your business or from forces outside of it.
- *Proactive change*: where you choose to make changes either to avoid future issues or to take advantage of future opportunities.

Clearly, the latter is preferable as it allows you to better plan what is needed and illustrates strong strategic management. Change that requires you to react means potentially you will have less time to plan and be less in control of the issues.

> We knew we would lose the Red Bull business at some point. The brand had grown to such a scale that it made sense for Red Bull to set up its own UK operation. However, it was a difficult situation for us to take charge. We didn't know when they would choose to do this and it made no financial sense for us to seize the initiative.

But whilst the change was predictable, we were not in any real state of readiness. We had discussed the issue many times but in spite of recognising the inevitability we had no plans in place to deal with the situation. Why? We had just been busy dealing with the day-to-day issues!

Managing successful change

In large corporations much of the emphasis on change management focuses on managing the process. Understandably, the process can be very complicated with large numbers of departments, people, functions, etc. However, anyone that has experienced this in large companies will sympathise with the view that the experience is often painful, especially for the rank and file. We suggest this is because there is too little emphasis placed on the management of the psychological issues that come into play in periods of uncertainty. In a small organisation the opportunity is to keep it simple; use uncomplicated processes and manage the mind-set of those around you. This can underpin successful change in a small company.

Let us consider therefore both these aspects:

1. the physical process
2. the psychology.

The process

A clear process is vital whatever the size of your organisation. It will give you a structured approach in what can be an uncertain time, whether you are a one man band or have people to manage. The process should be simple – a benefit afforded by the size of your company compared to that of a large organisation – and essentially follow normal planning criteria.

The psychology

At each stage of the process, your mind-set and that of those around you will potentially affect the success of the project. So alongside all the physical aspects of the process you need to think about how people will feel about it. The objective is to have all involved in a positive mind-set.

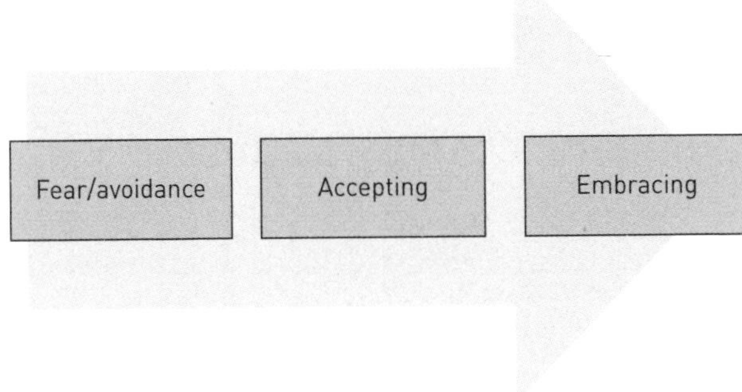

It is important to move from the position of fearing change to one where you accept it is a normal and important feature of your business life. If you are sitting in the position where you fear, or even worse, avoid change then you are putting your business in a very dangerous place. You will not be ready to make change. You will have less time to think through your options and will only ever be reactive to things that happen. As a result, you will not behave strategically.

Once you are in a frame of mind where you accept the need and role for change in your business, then you can be organised to manage it. You will be action orientated rather than avoidance seeking. You will be in a position of readiness.

Finally, being in a position of readiness to change can take you to a more enlightened level where you are attitudinally seeking positive change. Your attitude will be wholly positive (even in difficult circumstances) about your ability to orchestrate the necessary action.

The clear aim is to manage both the process and the psychology throughout the period of change.

Below we identify a simple six-stage change process:

	Process	Psychology
1 Be ready	The pre-requisite for success is to be in a state of readiness. Be alert for the problems and opportunities that may require you to implement change. This will enable you to be proactive and less reactive to issues. Raise the consciousness of things that affect your business both internally and externally. Achieve this through regular reviewing of your business on a monthly basis.	The way you feel about change will affect your own performance and have a halo effect on those around you. If you start from a position of reluctance you will be less successful and behind the game time wise. Psychologically, you need to be in position where you are at least accepting of the need to change and ideally be embracing change. Your attitude will cascade down to those working with you and ultimately influence their feelings too. Consciously raise change issues and encourage others to think proactively and creatively about solutions.
2 Be organised	Set your objectives first – what do you want to achieve. Construct a plan to meet the objectives. Keep it simple and focused. Clearly show what you need to achieve by when and by whom. Take particular care to consider both legal and employment issues. These are both areas that can be fraught with complexity and may justify some specialist advice.	If you are in the right frame of mind, you are more likely to create a positive set of goals for your plan. Embark on this task with enthusiasm and vigour – this will encourage others. You must communicate a sense of urgency and follow this up with your behaviour. Most change plans need to be executed quickly.
3 Get it out there	Arguably the most important stage. You need to bring on board those people who are affected by the change. You need to consider how and when to communicate the change details. This can be a difficult decision. Ensure that all communication is consistent and clear and not open to misinterpretation.	If you can include other stakeholders in the planning, they will be more likely to be committed to the plan. Be as open and honest as you can. Communicate face to face if possible. Whilst this may be uncomfortable for you, the effect on the other party will be significant. Talking face to face will invoke feelings of trust much more so than a letter or email. Never use text! The tone of communication is very important. Tone should be clear and calm.

4 Get on with it	Once you have communicated the plan, you need to move forward decisively and confidently into the implementation stage. Do not pontificate, as this will only suggest to those around you that you lack commitment to the plan. Ensure that everyone is clear on what is expected of them.	Keeping yourself and those around you motivated is key. Regular communication and updates will keep people informed and reassured. Ensure that you are seen to be fair in your decision-making. Keep face-to-face communication going. You may have to communicate bad news. Do not back away from doing this yourself. Those affected will usually understand if they feel that they have been treated with respect.
5 Keep going	Ensure that you closely monitor the process and that you are seen to do so. Issue regular updates on progress. Keep open channels of communications with all affected parties. Q & As can be very effective – ask for questions from individuals and then publish the answers to all.	Feeding back positive progress will keep everyone motivated. Communicating successes will ensure that morale is supported. Do not allow energy to dip as this will be felt emotionally as well.
6 Review and learn	You will not get everything right but if your business moves forward then you will likely have more change to manage in the future. Take the time to review your experiences so you will be ready next time.	After the event, share your feelings on the success and failures of the process. Ensure that others also get the chance to reflect on how by positively managing the process successful change was achieved.

Keeping a balanced approach to getting things done and managing the morale of those around you may not be easy but it will reap rewards. This will ensure that you, as the leader(s) of the organisation, and any other people within your organisation will come out of the change period in a positive frame of mind.

Periods of significant change can be exhausting as all your physical and emotional energies are focused on the processes. However, at the end of the process you need to be able to carry on with the business at hand. So a positive frame of mind is particularly important to also achieve the transition back to normal life.

The change situation we have outlined was particularly severe. We needed to radically alter the face of our business if we were to survive. We received help from our legal advisers and a great deal of support from our HR manager who, in particular displayed the skill of keeping morale high in the face of adversity.

We agreed with Red Bull a five-month transition period to manage the handover of the business to them. A transition team made up of members from both companies was put in place to ensure a smooth process.

Our priority was to establish our plan. We briefly considered closing the business but realised that in fact we didn't want to do that. We knew that we could scale back to a sustainable base. So we quickly established our goal: to create a restructured business that was financially viable, protect our employees, transfer Red Bull on time and to start enjoying life again.

This helped us realise that the problem had suddenly turned into an uplifting opportunity.

So we moved onto the planning stage with a sense of urgency – we needed to work the numbers quickly. Our big fear at this point was that news of the change would leak out of the Red Bull business. We did not want our employees or other major stakeholders to hear from anyone but us. We took the decision therefore to make an announcement whilst the planning stage was still going on.

We ensured that we had a simple but comprehensive announcement statement ready. Immediately prior to it's release:

- We called as many of our employees into a meeting as was possible.
- We had telephone conversations with our other brand owners.
- We had letters ready for customers.

We wanted to ensure that all immediate questions and concerns were directed at us to avoid mass speculation. We gave as much information as we could and were honest about not having all the answers yet. We gave our commitment to resolving the issues as soon as we could.

This allowed us to then draw on the extra resource we needed from our staff to complete the planning and start the process.

Over the next few weeks we tried to keep everyone informed, including lots of face-to-face meetings. We put in place a series of Q&As, which allowed everyone to ask questions and get a response. We resolved quickly what the staff structure for the downsized Ubevco would be, and asked Red Bull to do the same, and so were able to then put in place the processes for resolving the employment issues.

In the end, we transferred 60 people to the new Red Bull operation under the requirements of TUPE legislation (Transfer of Undertaking (Protection of Employment) Regulations), we established a new Ubevco team of around 60 people and unfortunately we had to make 10 people redundant. Everyone showed great spirit and fully cooperated with the process, especially those who knew that they probably wouldn't be working for the company in the future.

People respected that they were dealt with openly and honestly and it seemed to create an even stronger team spirit than had existed before.

"Change always comes bearing gifts."

Price Pritchett – organisational change expert

Key points

Whether the moment of change is planned or imposed, there is still a lot to be said for how you move forward through the change – managing the panic will only be achieved by effectively taking control.

- When bad news hits, whether it is expected or not, you need to find your position of power. This will ensure that you are not the victim and will reassure others that you are in control. Change makes everyone uncomfortable; if you present a positive picture of being in control, those around you will respond positively.
- Maintaining the trust of stakeholders is very important. To build and maintain trust you need to be as open and honest as you can be and to behave like this consistently. This can be achieved even when you don't have all the answers.
- In and of itself, being trustworthy and honest is a rewarding and uplifting state.
- If you say you are going to do something, make sure you do it. It keeps people believing. And if you can't deliver it, then tell people why.

The Red Bull situation could have crippled our business. We survived because strategically we had a very flexible financial model that allowed us to scale up and down quickly. We knew it would happen but did not have any specific contingency plans in place.

We had a lot of difficult decisions and a lot of uncomfortable meetings – people's livelihoods were at stake and it was understandable.

Our greatest learning was that by taking the decision to be open with people we earned their respect and trust. This is a valuable commodity. It made managing an uncertain situation not easier but much more rewarding.

Keeping information flowing gave people a sense of inclusion and although the detail of the information was not always complete and perfect, there was an acceptance that it was as good as it could be – and it gave us the time to get on with the important stuff.

The growth of the Red Bull brand had brought with it financial security and pressure. The Red Bull management was constantly applying pressure and our culture was being compromised.

The net result of the change was financially damaging in the short term but we came out the other side with a restructured and financially secure business. Our trade customers remained loyal. Our other brand owners were frankly delighted with the new circumstances, as they no longer felt in the shadow of Red Bull. And for all those staff that stayed in the Ubevco team the future looked a bit uncertain but definitely lighter and brighter.

So, it's true what they say, 'Red Bull gives you wings'!

TIPS

- *Keep information flowing:* this will have the effect of making people feel involved and informed.
- *Q & As really work:* ask people for their questions and then publish the answers. It endorses the sense of willingness to be open. Some people will be uncomfortable with asking questions themselves so they also provide reassurance to this group.
- *Face-to-face communication is best:* if you can, communicate all key information face to face rather than by letter or email. It might be uncomfortable for you but it will be more reassuring for the recipients.
- *Keep it simple:* focus communications on the simple stuff. People really want to know about how the changes affect them – whether customers, suppliers or employees.
- *Be legally astute:* don't take shortcuts on the legal issues. The law is there for a reason and it is easier (and cheaper) in the long term to follow it.

In summary

It is highly unlikely that all your planning assumptions will be accurate. Additionally, there will be things outside of your business that will require it to adapt and change.

- Change is a fact of life. There will be times when it affects our business requiring us to significantly alter our strategy and/or plan.
- At best, change can be planned for but very often the unknown influences from the environment outside of our control will mean that we need to react quickly.
- To manage change effectively we need to address both the process and psychological issues and put in place a plan to manage both.
- If you approach change with the right mind-set you will achieve it successfully, finding a new status quo which brings positives to your organisation.
- Change can be the impetus to readjust your business model to better suit the environment and you!

PART 4

UNCONVENTIONAL LESSONS

In writing this book we have tried to offer helpful guidance to the broad subject of starting a new business without pretending that we have all the answers. However, there is no substitute for the kind of real experiences we went through.

We have emphasised in the first three parts of the book that one of the main attractions of starting and owning your own business is that you can do things your way.

Throughout the 10 years that we ran our own company we were constantly learning. We found that as the years rolled by we developed our own mini-set of business theories that you are unlikely to find in any of the traditional "how-to-start-a-business" books on the market. We feel that there are a number of issues that are more relevant to the small business and should be treated differently. As such, they offer a less conventional set of guidelines but are illustrative of the kind of concerns or practices you may encounter.

- *Beware of experts.* We have discussed earlier where you might need to prudently use external experts to support your new venture. Here we offer some general words of caution that apply to all experts with regard to their own motivation and needs.
- *Luck or judgement.* All businesses will experience good and bad luck along the way – it is impossible to control everything that can affect the company. However, your attitude and judgement is very important in determining the impact that luck will ultimately have.
- *The do nothing strategy.* Can "doing nothing" really be an effective strategy for problem solving? We believe there are some very good reasons why it is.
- *Business bullies.* We have already discussed how to manage conflict in the context of your business relationships. Unfortunately, however, as a small business you may find yourself on the wrong side of a very powerful relationship. We had some direct experience of this and offer some reflections on how to best deal with it.
- *How to sleep at night.* Finally, there is a common perception that running your own business has to be a 24/7 job. We discuss the ways that enable the business owner to cope with the stresses associated with the job.

Chapter **18**

Beware of experts

In Chapter 9 we have outlined some circumstances in which you might need to take external advice to help start and develop your business. There are many occasions when selected advisers can be necessary and beneficial to your fledgling business. However, we also believe there are plenty of reasons to be cautious about the type and number of experts you use.

Reasons to beware of experts

1 Are they really "experts"?

The first question to consider is whether they are truly experts. These days it is fairly easy to garner public support that questions the expertise on offer, particularly from those involved in the economic and financial sectors. The global banking crisis that started in 2008 clearly showed that a significant proportion of the banking industry was taking unacceptable risks in the way they ran their businesses to the extent that it needed unprecedented government support to avoid a calamitous collapse of the whole financial system.

This apparent incompetence is not merely confined to the banking sector. Just read the broadsheet newspapers in their New Year editions each year, you will see that the "expert" predictions that they collate from various financial advisers and brokers show a huge range of opinion as to where things like the stock market indices will be in 12 months' time. If they were all experts, wouldn't you expect some unanimity in their opinions? Even less impressive is when you look back at what they predicted 12 months before and it seems clear that they have little better idea than any man in the street or indeed a pin stuck randomly in a chart. Perhaps the plain fact is that nobody can predict how the economic conditions will influence the financial markets – but if that is the case why do these financial institutions claim to be experts?

The majority of people, on the other hand, do tend to trust experts in other spheres. We are generally happy that airline pilots, doctors, dentists, bus drivers, and the like, are highly skilled in what they do and we will place our lives in their hands without any real trepidation.

So where is the distinction between such two groups of experts? It is hard to draw any conclusion other than that their motivations are different. Those that work in the "caring" professions are striving merely to perform their skilled tasks to ensure the safety and benefit of their customer, whereas arguably the primary objective of the other group is to maximise their own financial position whether or not this is to the detriment of their customers or society at large.

This is not to condemn all business experts, rather to emphasise that one should always bear in mind that when they are driven by financial motivation, their advice might be what is best for them rather than what is best for you.

2 They are not experts in your business

You are the expert in your business and no one, especially an outside consultant, can understand your business like you do. You need to work out precisely why you are bringing in an outside expert. If it is to undertake a specific function that either you do not have internally or that it is more efficient to outsource, fine. If, however, you want a consultant to look at more strategic issues then we would suggest that you take a step back and ask yourself if you are heading down the right path.

This is a common feature of corporate life. We have seen on numerous occasions large drinks companies purchase a new business or brand and then bring in consultants to help define the strategy. In our experience, as the distributor, we would then have to spend endless hours explaining to these "experts" how the sector operates. Using external consultants in the corporate world spreads the risk for the company executives who are responsible for the strategic development. Do not fall into this trap. If you have done your homework in terms of defining your proposition you should not need outside help on your strategy.

3 Lack of commercial realism

When dealing with external experts, it may not so much be that they are lacking in specialist skills, rather that they lack the ability to appreciate the relative importance of their particular issue in the context of the whole business. This is a very common problem when dealing with potential advisers across a range of activities.

One such simple example occurred when at Ubevco we were transferring our office lease. Some years before we had erected a short 10-foot wall to create a more aesthetically pleasing effect in our reception area. Alas, as we considered this insignificant, we had done it without the landlord's permission and the lawyer of the company taking over the lease raised this.

The wall was a simple wooden structure, costing only a couple of hundred pounds and could be taken down with any necessary licks of paint for the same amount of money or less. Yet the lawyer decided to go to town on this issue. First there were arguments about whether permission had been legally required or not under the terms of the lease, then about getting a belated lease amendment (which would have delayed the transaction and involved extra legal costs) and finally talk of getting external opinion about the costs of making good the illegal wall – which in any event the new tenants wanted to keep in place.

To end the nonsense we threatened to pull out of the deal unless the MD of the company taking it over just came to look at the wall and he did and within minutes agreed to instruct his lawyers to ignore the issue. Whilst the lawyer would argue he was acting thoroughly for his client, we would disagree and he incurred significant extra cost for everyone by not properly assessing the commerciality of the issue.

This kind of situation, where the external expert does not place the issue they are dealing with in an appropriate commercial context for your business, is very common. The legal profession can be particularly guilty of this in our experience, but so can your bankers, auditors and marketing specialists. Many such experts will not really have a full grasp of the relative commercial importance of factors within your particular business and this can affect the quality of the expert advice they can offer.

4 Where do their loyalties lie?

This is a similar issue to the earlier point about an expert's financial motivation, but also highlights some of the dangers of sharing your business intimacies with external experts.

Sometimes, advisers that you hire to guide you may prove to be less loyal than you would expect. You can find that the key confidant or expert suddenly switches their allegiance as circumstances change over time.

One particular example we encountered exemplified this kind of situation.

As product sales exploded, we had agreed eventually with Red Bull that we would recruit an extra specialist sales force to work solely on soft drinks. The Red Bull Company was concerned that the new people hired be a good cultural fit with the product image. This was not only a very time consuming exercise as it involved hiring 40–50 people, but also had the potential to be sensitive between our company and Red Bull. So we employed a recruitment specialist to manage the process and handle any sensitivities with Red Bull to ensure they were happy with the individuals recruited. The recruitment expert we chose we had used in our previous corporate life and so was very much 'our man'.

Some months later with a fully recruited team, the Red Bull Company advised that it would be setting up its own UK operation and would transfer all the newly created team to its payroll. This was not a total surprise of course, unlike the news that the head of our recruitment firm, our confidante and adviser, was now closing his firm and taking up a post working with Red Bull directly.

He would argue that he did nothing wrong and it was driven by financial need, but it still taught us that even advisers you believe are close to you may still be driven by self interest.

The lesson here is that you need to accept that any external expert that you use will ultimately be motivated by a number of things and your business is only a part of it. More realistically, the expert will be motivated by his/her own business needs both financial and otherwise and at the end of the day this could impact upon your business at some point. So, avoid becoming too reliant on individual/specific experts.

5 Experts are less receptive to innovative Ideas

There are schools of thought that experts are not the appropriate persons to assess your new and innovative business idea. There is a website, with no attributed author, fittingly called Beware of Experts (www.bewareofexperts.com) that forcefully makes the point that

> *"Experts are least suited to judge new excellent ideas*
>
> *It seems a perfectly rational approach to appoint experts to the task of evaluating and judging new ideas in any field of knowledge. The startling truth is that, as a group, experts in any field of knowledge are the least suited to identify excellent new ideas. Experts are the most likely to ridicule and dismiss as nonsense those ideas that depart farthest from their familiar body of knowledge and beliefs in any field of expertise. The majority of experts are rote learners devoid of creative juices. They possess a vast store of knowledge of facts, figures and detailed minutia of their particular field of expertise but lack the creative ability to venture outside the confines of their narrow field of knowledge and beliefs."*

The author believes that experts are guardians of the status quo and have a role to play, but it is not in their DNA to embrace new thinking or true innovation. He considers whether they could be trained to change but really concludes that you should fall back on your own conviction.

We believe that running a business is a lot simpler than some experts would like you to believe and that you stand most chance of succeeding if your business utilises your own personal strengths and experiences. You should be the expert in your business, using some support for noncore specialisations, but essentially making the key decisions yourself or with your business partners.

In summary

Experts are good in the following situations:

- when you need a specific professional service, e.g. legal, financial, tax;
- when you do not have the specific skill internally e.g. advertising;
- when you have an unusual circumstance where you feel particularly inexperienced.

But, you need to beware of experts, because:

- they are expensive;
- they have their own business agenda;
- their motivations may be different to your own;
- they do not understand your business like you do;
- they will be cautious which could constrain a new business.

Chapter 19

Luck or judgement

Perhaps the most common reason given for a small business's failure by the owners is that they were unlucky. One thing is for sure, luck will play a part in your new business life and dealing with it correctly might just be the difference between success and failure.

In our own business we certainly enjoyed our fair share of good and bad luck along the way. We believe that we survived in part due to the fact that we managed both circumstances to best effect. This enabled us to maximise the opportunity presented by good fortune and mitigate the negative impacts of the bad. How much of your success is due to the forces of luck versus the direct influence of your judgement is worthy of some thought.

What counts as luck?

So what is luck in a business context? The dictionary definition that perhaps best encapsulates it is:

> *The force that causes things, especially good things, to happen to you by chance and not as a result of your own efforts or abilities.*

In the business environment there is a whole raft of factors that are beyond your control, for example:

- the overall economic climate you are operating in;
- economic issues relating to you more specifically such as a fluctuating currency exchange rate or a regulatory tax;
- the behaviour of your customers and suppliers.

There is an inexhaustible list of things that can provide you with a lucky or unlucky break.

In circumstances which are out of your sphere of control, it is still important that you accept your power to manage the situation to best effect through good business judgement.

Coping with bad luck

The bad breaks you get in the course of running your business will generally be either:

1. specifically associated with your business and its commercial "playing field" – this might include a bad debt, losing a major customer, supplier letting you down, unexpected cost increases or loss of a key employee; or
2. wider occurrences that are really the result of chance factors in the world at large, such as floods, fires, power failures and such accidental events.

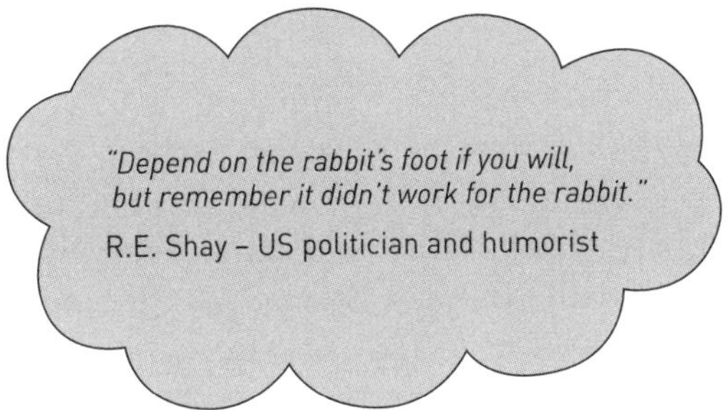

Whilst we would accept that in either case these situations do represent an unlucky break for your business, we nevertheless believe that these are assessable risks. With proper planning and management you should be able to limit the negative impact on your business, so that it can survive and wait for an opportunity to prosper at a later stage. So what are the keys to managing these risks?

We will consider first those events specific to your business. Probably the two most common events that owners blame for the failure of their company are that they incurred a major bad debt or that they lost their big customer. Sometimes, of course, both will occur at the same time.

As we have already touched upon in "Minimising risk", any bad debt is unfortunate but all too often they result from poor business judgement. It is absolutely fundamental for any business, particularly new and smaller ones, and so merits repeating. If you cannot manage the risk down to acceptable levels then you should not expose your business to the possibility of failure. We appreciate it is often easier to say that than do it, but look at whether you can get some credit insurance, the cost is usually worth it. Alternatively try and obtain some other form of security from your customer, or perhaps negotiate advance payments. Sharing your concerns with the customer can often find a solution that works for you both. Lastly, make sure your terms and conditions of sale allow you to keep legal ownership until such point as you have been paid for the products you sold.

Losing a key customer is a blow and can be precipitated by their financial failure. More often though it will be due to their changing ownership, a change in the key personnel, or other reasons arising from a change in the customer's own arrangements.

Over dependence on a single customer is a very common problem, and one that is not always readily solvable. Certain types of business by their very nature have few customers.

There was much media comment in 2011 regarding Bombardier's UK train making operation based in Derby. Firstly, it did not win a government contract worth £1.4 bn to supply trains for London Thameslink, which was controversially awarded to Siemens in Germany. This led Bombardier to announce that it would need to cut 1,400 of its 3,000 workforce, with its whole future in the balance if it failed to win either of the two next big contracts coming up in the ensuing 12 months. It is hard to see how life can be anything other than like this for such a specialised business dependent on very few but very large contracts being awarded.

A more relevant example would be an advertising agency or perhaps a professional consultancy. Individual entities like these tend to have relatively few clients and inevitably one or two are likely to have grown into being bigger clients than others and become a significant proportion of total income.

So what do you do? Turning down the business so that you do not become too dependent on it is rather self defeating. There are a number of protections you can put in place to help control this risk:

1 Work very hard to ensure you deliver an excellent service or product.

2 Negotiate with your customer a contract or agreement that gives you some period of notice in the event they want to leave you, and the longer the better.

3 Try and grow revenues from other customers too so as to diminish the reliance on your biggest one.

4 As you grow your business, make sure that you put in place mechanisms that can enable you to downsize in the event of the key customer loss.

5 If that is not feasible within your particular business genre, consider whether subcontracting production of the service or product might enable you to achieve the same flexibility.

6 Don't spend all your profits, save some for the rainy day.

7 React swiftly to any potential or actual changes in ownership of your customers. This will give you the best chance of winning over the new proprietors. Engage the support of the previous owners where possible.

It is not just the loss of a major customer that can be bad luck, if you are dependent on a key supplier exactly the same concerns are likely to apply.

The nature of our business at Ubevco was more akin to a consultancy or agency in that we had "clients" or brand owners who we represented and sold their goods on to our customers. We have discussed in prior chapters how we dealt with losing our biggest client but, of course, it serves us well here as an example of surviving a major "unlucky" event!

At Ubevco the huge explosion of Red Bull sales meant that even though our other sales had more than doubled, by the year 2001 over 85% of our turnover came from sales of Red Bull. We had achieved widespread distribution and had over 400 customers to whom we sold for onward sale into shops, bars and the like. But our client or supplier could take away our distribution rights at any time at four months' notice despite our best efforts over the years to negotiate a longer contract.

The key message is that whilst it obviously had a massive impact on our financial performance, we were able to survive

and later thrive again because we had contingency planned for the eventuality.

What about when the bad luck is from the world at large rather than your own particular business environment? This would include floods, plagues, power failures and such other accidental occurrences that might impact on your ability to perform your business tasks and produce your income. Again, the key is to assess the risks as part of your overall business planning.

This will immediately suggest taking some sensible precautions, the simplest but vitally important example being with your computer systems and records. The need to properly back up your systems is pretty well known by users everywhere nowadays. Equally, a device that protects your main server or computer from power surges and gives you power after a cut for sufficient time to orderly close down the system is a good protection for any business as such breakdowns can frequently cause loss of data.

You should consider all the vulnerabilities that your business has to physical accidents outside your control. There are two sources of help that should ensure you get this right. The first is through your business insurance. Whether or not you use a broker or buy this online, the review of your coverage should prompt you to consider what you can do to protect your income stream against such acts of business interruption. There are a number of insurances any business should consider, as we already have touched on in Chapter 10. Rather cheerfully, these are likely in this context to include whether you need "key man" insurance which is designed to provide funds to support a business whose key management/owner is unable to continue working through incapacity or death.

You will probably also get help through your finance provider. Nearly all banks will now discuss with you what measures and insurances you have in place to protect your business against these types of circumstance. This is part of their due diligence to protect their lending, but can be a helpful checkpoint for you.

TIP Utilise your insurer or bank to help assess risk of business interruption.

As regards non-physical concerns, such as the wider adverse economic conditions, we have previously suggested that these can arguably present as many opportunities as problems. One of your great strengths as a small business is that you can move quickly and nimbly to react to these circumstances. So try and seek the positives in these situations and act decisively to take advantage of them.

So our message is clear, there is no doubt that bad luck can hamper your business and make it less successful for a time than you might wish. However, if you make the right judgement calls when you encounter it and have planned for possible scenarios, you should be able to limit the damage that misfortune can inflict. Moreover, you will be in position to prosper again when circumstances turn in your favour.

Bad luck as a stimulant for change

Glib clichés can sometimes be really annoying and perhaps one such irritant is:

> *What doesn't kill you makes you stronger.*

And frankly we don't even think that it's true very often. However, there are many examples of where a stroke of misfortune has precipitated a change in strategy that has ultimately helped a business move on to greater success.

Although we will not labour the point again here, one needs to look no further than one of the central themes of this book, namely that you can turn the bad luck of your redundancy into a positive and successful business life change.

Sir Alf Ramsey was the manager of the only English football team to win the World Cup. As an example of bad luck being a catalyst for successful change, the story of England's win provides one of the best. At the time, England's greatest goal scorer was

Jimmy Greaves, regarded as one of the best players in the world and the man on whom their hopes of winning seemed to rest even though England struggled through the first games of the tournament. Unfortunately for Mr Greaves he got injured in one of these games and his replacement, the largely untried Geoff Hurst, took his place. The team played better, started winning and Mr Hurst became the first player to score three goals in the final. He is now Sir Geoff Hurst whereas poor Jimmy is left to still handle questions about how he felt nearly 50 years later.

Was this just a lucky break for England, probably, but for sure it was a catalyst for change and the manager exercised great judgement in how he resolved the problem. It is again a question of taking the positive out of any situation. A stroke of bad luck may well produce a need for you to re-think or change a business model or philosophy and if you manage it properly it can often be for the good. There may be some shorter term pain due to the loss of income or extra cost, but the change may be beneficial in the longer term.

Finding good luck – and using it!

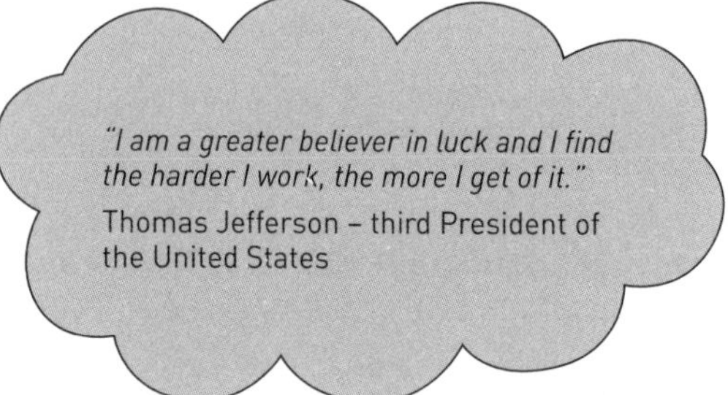

Mr Jefferson was one of many "lucky" people who have proffered this notion in various guises. We certainly concur with his sentiments.

Your business has a much better chance of finding lucky breaks if you:

1. are alert to opportunities
2. work harder and more attentively that your competition

3 then convert the opportunity through your expertise.

There are some famous examples of where a company has been perceived to have been very lucky. Invariably though we would contend they have exercised great judgement and used a combination of these three facets. It's easy with hindsight to accuse them of just being lucky.

Many people have chronicled the history of Microsoft and its remarkable ascent to the position it now holds in the business world. It is often held to have been lucky and, of course, on occasion it was, but Microsoft certainly made the big decisions count when presented with this good fortune. Perhaps the best example of how it capitalised on some good luck with some great management and strategy was in its initial dealings with IBM over the latter's DOS system. Microsoft was anxious not to become too dependent on one customer but IBM was the pivotal contract it needed.

Microsoft realised that IBM had become embroiled in antitrust legislation at that time, which gave Microsoft an opportunity to steer IBM away from the kind of royalty deal that it usually demanded and instead to just charge Microsoft a one-off fee. This allowed Microsoft to keep the rights to be able to license the product elsewhere. Consequently, in due course Microsoft was able to license the DOS software to IBM PC clones and, moreover, this became the model for how Microsoft would sell its software for years. It was lucky that IBM was in a difficult position at that time, but Microsoft took advantage of the luck brilliantly.

In this example, the good luck did not just fall into Microsoft's lap; really it just exercised great judgement in identifying that the opportunity existed. This is an important distinction and it is often very easy to be unaware that a fortunate set of circumstances exists that can help your business.

A small but good example we were involved in demonstrates that everyday diligence can find you a piece of luck ahead of your competition and therefore take better advantage. It occurred where we benefited from a good-luck change in legislation with Tiger Beer. For years all imports from Singapore had attracted an import tax (on top of normal

duty) of 12%. Our sales at the time were hampered by the fact that some of the specialist wholesalers selling into the Asian restaurant industry in the UK were importing their beer direct from contacts in Asia rather than from us. Tucked away in the budget legislation one year was a removal of this import tax and because we were thorough always in reviewing the detail of any budget, we immediately were able to reduce our cost by the 12%, and the Asian wholesalers consequently started buying from us rather than import themselves. A second benefit was that we could now compete more effectively against the competitive set of beers that Tiger was up against. This good fortune helped us on two fronts, but without our awareness and quick reaction, only one of these benefits would have been enjoyed.

You hear people talking about being in the right place at the right time, or getting their timing right but these are really no different to points we are making about finding good luck. We firmly believe that if you have some forethought and regularly put yourself in the right places, you will get these good breaks. Without doubt though it's good to enjoy the good ones early on in your career as a business owner, as it can arm you better to deal with the bad ones.

In my early career at a UK ad agency I recall one evening out with some young colleagues we were blessed with the presence of our chairman who was a well established agency principal. Keen to make a good impression, one of the copywriters asked him what was the best piece of business advice he could give to anyone. Before the chairman could reply, the inquisitor excused himself and went to the toilets, and so didn't hear that 'Timing is everything' was the biggest lesson our chairman had learned in his business life. This, of course, led to much hilarity but there was no better way to reinforce the message.

Chris

In our view, how you deal with your good luck should not be very different with how you deal with your bad luck. The more considered you are, and the better your business judgement and ensuing decisions, the greater will be the benefit you derive from your lucky breaks. The key is not to waste these strokes of good fortune, and if you are properly applying all the principles that you have adopted to run your business, then you should maximise the return you get.

We have set out our strong conviction here that you can influence your chances of getting good business luck, and the impact of good or bad luck will be defined by how well you have prepared for it and manage it. This is our very Western culture and style, but as you know from our musings on culture one should always appreciate and recognise the beliefs of others. Our final example on the subject of luck or judgement illustrates how this awareness can pay dividends:

Luck and superstition

In many cultures and religions there is a firm belief that luck is not a matter of random chance but rather can be explained as a product of their faith or superstition. As importers of Tiger Beer, we dealt with all the major UK predominantly Asian owned wholesalers into the Asian food and drink markets. In Asia, the number 8 is regarded as lucky and associated with good fortune and prosperity. The number 4, on the other hand, is considered to be very unlucky, with its association with the word death, and is frequently avoided in product lines. Nokia for instance skipped the '4' series in its phone range. To pay respect to this, we arranged for the Ubevco phone numbers to include as many '8's as possible and no '4's. So we had 880028, which was the best we could negotiate with BT. This may seem like an inconsequential action, but it was commented favourably upon by all our Asian customers and helped strengthen our bond with these important business partners.

In summary

We have included the subject of good and bad luck in this book because there is no doubt that it can influence your business. However we believe that exercising good business judgement will not only influence the likelihood of getting better luck, but also will dictate how it affects your business. You can ride out periods where the external factors have worked against you by good management and being prepared, and be no worse off than a business that has enjoyed some good luck but failed to take best advantage. The most successful businesses will have taken maximum advantage of their good luck by making great decisions alongside these fortunate breaks. Conversely, the least successful will be those ventures that compound any misfortune by also taking bad decisions.

Chapter **20**

The do nothing strategy

Throughout this book we see a good selection of the ups and downs associated with being at the helm of your own business. Possibly the greatest advantage and at the same time the biggest disadvantage is that the buck stops with you. At the end of the day, the final decision on any issue is yours. You may seek counsel from others both inside and outside the organisation but in the end it is important that any decision you take sits comfortably with you. The upside of this coin is that you can make decisions that fit well with your own ethos. The flipside is that you can't blame some faceless corporation for your behaviour.

Decision-making can be a very lonely aspect of running a business. Sometimes it is hard to share the big issues affecting the company with those working for you.

We were lucky at Ubevco. There were three equal partners each bringing different experience and perspective to the table and each prepared to be full and forthright with their views. We had many "healthy" debates along our journey. But at least it was certainly not a lonely road to decision making. Nevertheless, there were many occasions when we found it difficult to make a decision.

It was not unusual that we would have spent several hours discussing a problem or issue and having been round the options a few times simply could not find a way forward. We came to call this the "*do nothing strategy*".

"So we are agreed then, we won't do anything."

On the surface, this may look like we were simply unable to reach agreement and in the early days sometimes that is how it felt. Surely, having identified an issue or problem it is wrong not to take action to resolve it? Well over time, we realised the result of inaction can be positive. We came to understand that in certain situations "doing nothing" is the correct course of action and it became therefore an important part of our decision-making tool kit.

The do nothing strategy in simple terms is the conscious managerial decision to not take any action. By definition, therefore, it is a decision and this differentiates it from just avoiding the problem.

As with all good strategy there is a thought process that leads to the "do nothing" decision. In order to reach the decision that you should take no action, you need first to fully explore the issue or problem. It is very important that the problem is correctly identified and understood. Doing nothing just because you don't really understand the issue is not appropriate – ever. If you don't understand the problem, then there is a need to take action to ensure that it is investigated further.

However, once a problem has been correctly identified and fully reviewed, you will be in a position to explore the options for resolution. Again, it is important that exploring the options is done with vigour.

When you have identified all the available courses of action, you are in the position to decide which can solve your problem. It is at this point that we would propose there are some situations where you may wish to deploy the do nothing strategy:

1. where any or all of the possible solutions may not be good for your business
2. where the solution may create a different problem
3. where the solution is not financially viable
4. where there may not be a solution
5. where you may simply not have the experience to find a solution
6. where it is impossible to predict the outcome
7. where there is a strong probability that the problem will go away in time.

The key point is that sometimes if you take action you may be responsible for making things worse. Let's consider these points in a little more detail.

1 The solution is not good for your business

The best example we can draw on is the Red Bull company's demands for more people.

> By early 1999, the brand was growing exponentially. We had slowly but surely increased our headcount to just over 50 people and were covering all the bases in terms of trade customers. But in spite of this and the clear success of the brand, Red Bull's management was obsessed with increasing the headcount further. We had many internal debates about this. We didn't feel there was a need to add

more people, we were concerned about the distraction caused by recruitment and financially we didn't see any benefit, just more risk. So we decided to do nothing. Increasing the headcount didn't seem to be good for the business at that point.

This was undoubtedly the right action at the time. We quadrupled brand volume in that year.

Unfortunately, we were not able to sustain this position. By the end of 1999, the pressure from Red Bull increased and we would have harmed the relationship significantly had we taken no action. The problem had changed and we needed to react differently to it.

2 The solution creates a different problem

Sometimes, a solution to a short-term issue can just create another problem elsewhere.

In the alcohol category, the majority of sales will have been made with the duty already paid to the government. So, typically, Ubevco would pay the duty on all its beers before it went into the trade. There is a sector known as the under-bond market where the stock is kept in warehouses and the duty isn't paid until it is sold out of the warehouse. There are specialist companies that operate in this sector. As a result, the prices into these customers are lower than into other sectors as the customer becomes responsible for paying the duty.

We were sometimes asked by brand owners to sell into this sector, as the volume was in theory incremental. However, we knew that selling into this sector carried risks:

1 The volume would not be sold in the UK but shipped abroad into another market and create problems for another distributor.

2 It could be re-imported illegally without payment of any duty.

3 Rumours of lower pricing would circulate with the broader base of customer.

On this basis, we felt that if we sold into this sector we were potentially creating a different problem down the line. This problem would be much more difficult to manage and so took the decision that it was not in the best interests of the business.

3 The solution is not financially viable

This is probably the easiest and most frequent example of using the do nothing strategy. Throwing money at a problem is sometimes a very valid way of solving a problem. However, it is also true that self evidently this can be an expensive route to problem resolution and therefore dangerous both in terms of your financial position and in terms of establishing precedents.

One of the problems we regularly experienced as a small player in a large competitive market was the excessive demands of the big retailers for promotion activity, which of course they expect the supplier to fund.

The large brands regularly ran promotions in the main supermarkets that sold product below cost. Why? Well often their objectives were more aligned to corporate share than normal profitability. However, this often led to the buyers asking for similar promotions from smaller players too. We managed to sidestep these demands in the early days by just claiming to be too small but as our business grew this got harder to justify.

The dilemma came when finally one of the supermarkets threatened to delist our brand if we didn't run a very deep cut-price promotion. Financially, this promotion made no sense but losing the distribution would have also been difficult. In the end, we held our position. The customer was nonplussed for a while but didn't delist the product. This brand actually performed quite well and delisting it didn't make sense to the retailer. It was an uncomfortable situation the first time we encountered it but doing nothing in this situation was definitely the best decision. It gave us the confidence when this issue reoccurred many times!

4 There may not be a solution

Problems are complicated and the possible solutions may not be within your control. Sometimes you just have to accept that you are unable to solve the problem and so taking action will be futile or possibly make the situation worse.

Even after running our business for 10 years we came across problems that we simply couldn't find an answer to. Occasionally, this was where brand owners were asking for information that was simply impossible to supply without hiring a psychic. Or sometimes where the issue was so great, taking action would only bring about the inevitable sooner.

> Having doubled the size of our headcount and set up separate beer and soft drink teams, the issue of culture in the organisation became very challenging.
>
> In one part of the business we had a strong Ubevco culture, which we felt underpinned our success and in another part we had an emerging Red Bull culture that was not only different but also arguably counter to our own. This was a very uncomfortable period.
>
> To solve this problem would have meant squashing the Red Bull culture within Ubevco, which would have created problems with our relationship with the Red Bull Company. So we did nothing. Eventually, Red Bull decided to take the distribution in house and the problem was solved for us!

5 Insufficient experience

The do nothing strategy also has a place on occasions that are not wholly related to problem solving. Sometimes you discover a new opportunity for your business. If this situation is within the remit of your experience, then all is well and good. If this is not the case, then there is an argument that caution should prevail.

> Sometimes it's your own colleagues who have the greatest capacity to surprise and expose your own inexperience. One such example occurred in early 2001 when our sales

director discovered that one of our regional Red Bull sales managers was on the shortlist of 24 contenders to appear on the next series of Channel 4's *Big Brother*. At the next management meeting there was mild panic. Did he need permission? Could we deny him permission? Would we pay him whilst he was 'in the house'? What if he went all the way and was missing for 12 weeks? What might he say on air about Ubevco and his colleagues? What might he say about Red Bull? Should we tell Red Bull? Who would do his work? The questions went on and on. None of this was helped by the fact that the individual concerned, although highly competent, was something of a 'character' – just what *Big Brother* was looking for!

Of course, we had no prior experience to draw upon to help answer these questions so we decided to do nothing and wait for the sales manager to bring the problem to us. We trusted that he might offer solutions to our concerns at the same time, guided one would hope by the programme producers who did have experience in this unusual situation. Somewhat sadly, he fell at the final hurdle and didn't make the final 12.

6 Where there is no predictable outcome

This is possibly the worst kind of problem. Even when you go through a rigorous process of assessing your problem and identifying the options, you will from time to time find yourself in the situation where you cannot predict the outcome from the proposed actions.

It may be more appropriate to call this the "buying yourself time" option as waiting before taking action can allow you to answer the questions around predictability.

In 2002 we started working with a brand called Mike's Hard Lemonade.

We were in the post-Red Bull era and keen to build the portfolio again. Mike's Hard Lemonade was a vodka premix product with 'attitude'. It was very successful in both USA and Canada and the brand personality had a

good fit with our own. We were trying to move quickly in order to get into the trade for the important summer period. All was going to plan until a government imposed change in duty rates meant that producing the drink with malt alcohol rather than the original vodka base would significantly lower the product cost. The premium brands in the UK generally used vodka but this change gave other malt produced brands a significant price advantage. Our difficulty was that we did not have the means of predicting what would happen within the trade but as we were under time pressure to go ahead with the launch we plumped for staying with the more expensive vodka based product.

The right option would have been to wait – do nothing – until we were able to predict the outcome. Time would have allowed us to do some research which undoubtedly would have given us the answer. The result was we went ahead with the launch and lost a great deal of money on stock that simply we couldn't sell.

7 Where there is a strong probability that the problem will go away in time

Doing nothing is sometimes very scary even if you know it is the right thing to do. In these situations it is important to focus on the important things.

Once Red Bull had broken through as a new and exciting brand, it was inevitable that there would be a period where 'me too' competitors would enter the fray. In fact, 15 years on we are still seeing 'new' and 'exciting' Red Bull lookalikes trying to get a piece of the action. Amongst the dozens of brands appearing on the scene there were a few who had a serious strategy and targeted Red Bull in its heartland. Basically, their strategy was to offer high investment to replace Red Bull on the basis that the account would continue to sell their product at the same rate. In these situations, we had trade customers come back to us asking us to match the competitor offering or be delisted.

We knew that the strength of the Red Bull brand was greater than the rival set but the threat of delisting is never comfortable. Fortunately, we were very much supported and encouraged by the Red Bull Company not to take any action in these situations. We did encourage customers not to take Red Bull out completely but to put the rival alongside Red Bull if they were determined to take the investment from the rival brand and many did this. Others though took Red Bull out. In a relatively short period of time the vast majority of all customers returned Red Bull to its previous status. And the brand was stronger having proved its superior status.

Had we conceded in these circumstances, we would have undermined the brand equity and invested marketing money in unnecessary and inappropriate ways.

In summary

The do nothing strategy can be an effective tool to have in your decision-making tool box.

- As the business owner, it is ultimately up to you to deal with the issues and problems that occur in your business.
- Sometimes doing nothing is a better option and much less risky than doing something.
- It is important that the issue has been properly assessed and that the decision to take no action is taken because it produces the best solution at that time for your business.
- Doing nothing is a decision!

Chapter 21

Business bullies

In today's world bullying gets a lot of press and is seriously frowned upon, whether as a feature of the playground or the workplace.

We understand bullying in the workplace mainly in the context of the over zealous boss in his management of co-workers. Within a small company this is relatively easy to manage through the encouragement of good cultural values.

Bullying is basically about the abuse of power, the stronger abusing the weaker. A small business is likely to work with larger organisations and managing the power equation is just a fact of life. However, this is an area where small businesses can also find themselves in situations where they are vulnerable to more overt bullying by more powerful organisations.

Business bullying we would argue is a cultural issue. You will certainly not find it amongst any listed espoused values and yet there are clear examples that the behaviour is used so consistently in some organisations it implies that it is part of the deeper set of behaviours that make it cultural.

Fundamentally, this is a moral issue. Why do organisations with strong morally based values also allow bullying – it is a silent but very sinister trait.

What do we mean by business bullying?

It is difficult to accurately define where the use of power in a business relationship crosses the line. In the main, this is seen as fair in the love and war world of a capitalist society. The strongest will win and we shouldn't confuse this with bullying.

Of deeper concern, is the more extreme situation where the use of power goes beyond the boundaries of what is normally accepted as moral. These situations include unnecessary aggression and threats, withholding money, lying and cheating for business gain when it is related to the power of the large organisation over a smaller one.

We could write a book of examples but the point of this section is not to avenge but to forewarn.

One of the primary objectives of our Ubevco business was to gain widespread distribution for our drinks brands.

This meant selling to the big players in the UK drinks markets: the brewers, the pub companies, national cash and carry chains and of course the big supermarket groups.

Most of our worst experiences were with companies from the supermarket sector. One of the most extreme examples occurred after the distribution contract we had with Red Bull moved over to the Red Bull's own UK company at the end of 2001. We had negotiated a written agreement with one of the key supermarkets that it would receive a bonus of £30,000 should it achieve a certain volume of sales of Red Bull during a period that ended on 31 December 2001 – our last day of selling Red Bull. The supermarket missed this volume sales target, not by a bit but by a country mile! These things happen. Volume incentives are meant to be challenging and encourage the seller to give better shelf space, etc. to your product, and to that extent are a cost that usually comes out of the marketing budget.

The supermarket in question, despite being aware that it had missed the incentive target, proceeded to raise its own paperwork internally – a 'debit note' and promptly knocked off £30,000 plus VAT from the payment that it owed Ubevco for the supply of product. Needless to say, we complained to the supermarket, respectfully pointing out that there was no reason or even mitigating circumstances as to why the supermarket should be entitled to the £30,000.

One might already consider that the deducting of the money itself constituted a bullying attitude by the supermarket. However, things got worse. Ubevco needed to demonstrate to the beer brands we represented that we would be able to continue to grow their sales with our newly scaled down business. The supermarket chain threatened that unless we honoured the £30,000 debit note that it had raised it would de-list our beers from its stores – nearly all our beer products sold well in the chain's numerous stores.

In other circumstances, we might have called their bluff, but the business was at such a sensitive stage that we could not risk the beer de-list and so gave in and paid the £30,000.

Red Bull quite rightly refused to pay its share, and so we had to pay it in full – it meant that we could afford to employ one person less for 2002.

Was this extreme case of business bullying down to the errant activities of one buyer or a product of that particular company's own culture? At that time we certainly believed it was the latter.

A few years later another supermarket chain announced the day after Budget Day that the Chancellor's alcohol duty increases constituted a price increase by the supplier and therefore they would not accept them unless and until their buyer had met with the supplier's representative. This was contrary to the Chancellor's budget speech where he specifically asked for the increase to be applied through the supply chain immediately.

Moreover, the supermarket advised that no appointments to meet their buyers would be available for a couple of months. It gave beer suppliers the option of being de-listed if they did not wish to absorb the duty increase themselves until such time as they could negotiate with their buyers. A few brave suppliers were duly de-listed. We will leave you to draw your own conclusion whether this is fair play, or the abuse of power.

At the other extreme, the British brewers, equally as powerful, would always negotiate hard and in some ways were more difficult to gain a listing with, largely because they had their own products as a priority. However, they never adopted bullying tactics, they paid on time and didn't claim things they were not entitled to.

After Tiger Beer UK took over the business, Ubevco still had to collect the outstanding monies owed to us by customers.

We ended up having to take legal action against just three of these many hundreds of companies, all major supermarket chains. In one case, the money owed was only about £15,000 and related to just two invoices for delivered goods. After months and months of normal chasing methods and legal letters and demands, we finally took them to court and won the legal judgment that the money was due in full as claimed.

The supermarket chain concerned then refused to pay the legal judgement demanding fresh paperwork, despite it already having being sent many times, including by recorded delivery as part of the legal process. Our lawyers wouldn't send it, advising that we were now entitled to issue a seven-day winding up order (because a court order was unpaid) on one of Britain's biggest supermarkets. Only then did they see fit to pay us the £15,000 and our costs!

We were only able to take such action because we no longer needed to trade with them – can you imagine the repercussions had we still been trying to sell them beer?

It is fair to say that in recent years there is an increasing emphasis on corporate responsibility and we would hope that newly formed businesses will encounter much less of this type of behaviour than we did. Nevertheless, it is best to be aware of the possibilities.

In summary

In any situation, it is unpleasant to feel bullied or treated unfairly in some way. In certain trade sectors there seems to still exist situations where the power of the large organisation is wielded unfairly on the smaller party. Whilst you cannot stop this happening you still have the power to take some actions.

- Through your own culture you can encourage good communication – this can help to defend against certain types of underhand behaviour by being diligent and precise and encouraging written agreements with suppliers and customers.
- Encourage open communication internally so that employees feel able to bring these problems to you.

- If you can, have good legal advice/support so you understand the ramifications of defending yourself properly.
- Be clear yourself about where to draw the line. Sometimes you have to take the extreme position of withdrawing from the relationship.

Chapter **22**

How to sleep at night

How do you sleep at night with all the responsibilities of a business is a question you may well be asking.

There will be times, of course, when you feel under pressure. You are dependent on the success of your business, for your own livelihood and if you take on employees you are responsible for theirs too. Many of the suggestions we have made throughout the book should give you confidence that you can manage the pressures, both financial and otherwise.

1 Manage your personal pressure

Way back in Part 1, we discussed the value of having a fall-back plan for your personal finances, managing the risk and thereby knowing you can find a way through it as far as your family finances are concerned. We have also suggested that you should make sure you manage and limit your exposure to personal guarantees. If you have built a business of substance with employees, you will almost certainly be structured as a limited company, which in itself helps limit your personal financial exposure.

2 Take a long-term view

The feast and famine parables hold good in business and if you use the good years to help bolster the financial strength of your business then you can often survive the bad ones.

> At Ubevco we had grown our business to a turnover of £105m just four years after starting up, only to find one July day that we would be losing £90m of that turnover in a few months. We are probably prouder of our achievement in surviving that loss than we were of getting to £105m in the first place. We have used this example elsewhere to illustrate how to manage change, risk and the benefits of outsourcing but all of these relate to the same key point. We managed the business with one eye on the downsides. Consequently, the night after we got the news, we slept soundly.

3 Focus on cash flow

Probably the biggest single factor that causes stress for a business owner is where you cannot pay your bills. The root cause of this can often be much broader and is a consequence of your business running unprofitably. The remedial action in these cases lies in reassessing your business plan and making the changes you need to steer the business back on course to profitability.

Just as often though the cause of cash flow problems can lie not in the underlying performance of the business but simply in poor management of your finances. No matter how long you have been in business, you should always focus a lot of attention on efficient cash management. Typically, this is making sure your customers pay you on time, and if your business holds stocks of product, making sure you don't tie up too much money in excess inventory. We have illustrated how debtor collections can sometimes be best managed by outsourcing (maybe factoring) but however you choose to deal with this issue, it should always be one of your very top priorities.

This will then enable you to pay your creditors on time, which will in the long term have a positive effect on the reputation of your business and strengthen your negotiating position.

In my early corporate career there seemed a general acceptance that smart financial management involved holding onto your company's cash as long as possible by paying people as late as you could. It almost seemed that this was how you earned respect as a financial officer and too much focus was on slowing creditor payments rather than on getting your debts collected quickly. It's hard to understand now why that was the case, and I am convinced that being able to pay your suppliers promptly is the best sign that you are running an efficient business. Fortunately, most (but certainly not all!) bigger corporations are beginning to take this view too and it has become less acceptable to deliberately not pay to terms.

Chris

4 Setting your goals

It is all too easy to just focus on financial performance and pressures. These were not necessarily the primary goals you identified when you were considering leaving employment in the first place. We have discussed the benefit of setting realistic goals for you as you start up in business. As time goes by it can be easy to forget these, especially when the business has changed with circumstances and has maybe moved in a different direction or to a different scale than you first envisaged.

There is of course nothing wrong with re-assessing and amending your goals over time, especially when you have already achieved your initial aims. Quite often you may feel pressurised about achieving some current target or solving some problem within your business, but forget to look back at the reasons you started it in the first place. When you do, you will hopefully realise that these current pressures are still preferable to your old working life.

5 Staying true to your values

Whether you formalised these or not at the start of your business, you will have a set of underlying values that you sought to bring into your new venture. These may have been a response to some of the frustrations you had with the way things were done in your life as an employee or just an inherent part of your character. Either way, one of the greatest satisfactions you will get from running your own operation will be from knowing that you have stayed true to these values.

This might be exemplified by the way you treat your employees, or customers and suppliers. The goals that you set for your business are usually definable targets, and the achievement of them is a major source of pride. Knowing that you have met these goals by running the business in the manner and style that you set out to employ is arguably just as rewarding.

Winning is fun, and in business achieving your goals is winning, but not at any cost. The enjoyment you get from business ownership will equally come from staying true to your own values – whatever they might be for you and any business partners.

6 Achieving the right work/life relationship

As you call the shots in your business you will hopefully have found that you can better accommodate some of your personal life aspirations. Being able to choose your own location and work hours can have a hugely beneficial effect on your personal life. Tailoring your work hours to suit your own purposes is a further massive benefit from being the boss. There are other less tangible aspects that can positively influence your piece of mind. You do not need to be an egotist to feel an extra sense of worth and pride in being the owner of business. People will tend to perceive you with added respect and you may have the opportunity to further enhance your reputation in the local community.

If you are better able to manage the home/work balance, you will hopefully have a sense of making a stronger commitment to your family and friends. Often a long and stressful career in the corporate world can lead to alienation from home.

Running your own business gives you two opportunities that should help you sleep at night. Firstly, a sense of being able to make a greater contribution at home and reconnecting with your family. Secondly, you may also have a business, which will begin to feel like a family too, irrespective of whether your family are actually involved, or not.

Ubevco soon came to feel like a family. Some of our employees were with us for the duration of the company. We got to know many of them very well and over time often their families too.

The family atmosphere was boosted from time to time as one or other of our families were called upon to help.

Pete, Catherine's brother-in-law, gave us a lot of help in the early days, enabling us to have exhibition stands and conference staging which was greater than our purse strings would allow at the time.

Stephen, Chris's son, spent a few months working in the logistics team for some work experience and gaining great insight into working in a female-only team along the way.

And, Karen, Chris's very patient wife, helped us out on many occasions, especially looking after the office whilst the rest of the company escaped on a company conference. And it is very doubtful that she ever received any recompense for her trouble!

7 Start planning your exit

As you and your business mature, you can begin to think about your exit from the business. This probably won't mean a return to being an employee if you have come this far, but rather a well earned retirement or perhaps even to a new and different start-up. Many owners favour a gradual retreat whereby they reduce their working commitment over time as family members or existing colleagues take over the management of the business. This often means you can retain some of the ownership and thereby earn some income. Alternatively, a complete exit can be achieved in a number of ways:

- passing on the ownership or management to family or colleagues
- outright sale or merger with a third party
- winding up the operation.

As our primary purpose in this book is to encourage employees to become entrepreneurs, we will not focus on exit strategies other than to say that as things have settled down, having some exit options in your mind and beginning to plan for them will be sensible. We know from our own experiences that it may not always be possible to achieve your first choice option – the multi-million pound sale may appeal to you but not to any buyers – so in many instances it is likely that you will need to consider more than one way of effecting your exit.

Either way, planning for your exit will at some stage need to come into your thinking and often will be another cause for satisfaction that you can see the whole project through.

In summary

So in conclusion, provided you don't drink too much Red Bull in the evenings, we see every reason why you should sleep contentedly and soundly at night throughout your time as a business owner. As you stay true to your values, the satisfaction that most people feel from running their own operation far outweighs some of the extra pressures, and the majority do not return to the life of an employee. You will be able to cope with the occasional stresses and pressures that any business encounters provided you:

- set yourself realistic goals
- keep things in perspective
- actively manage your cash flow
- manage prudently, sensibly and simply
- manage the work/life balance so that you enjoy both.

Conclusions

In our introduction to this book, we set out to achieve the following:

- to explain why the option of business ownership is very achievable for many people with a corporate background;
- to offer guidance on the process of moving from employee to entrepreneur;
- to use our own experience to illustrate both the issues that arise and importantly the key benefits that come with owning your own business.

Hopefully, as you have worked through the four sections of the book you have found answers to some of your questions and if not, have a better idea of where to go and get them.

The big bits of advice

We have attempted to pass on many of the relevant lessons we learned along the way. When we condense our thoughts, there a few big bits of advice that we think were the key to our success:

1. *Experience is invaluable.* Your own unique experience as an employee makes you highly skilled. If you find a business concept that utilises these skills, you are giving yourself the best chance to succeed. Moreover, your prior experience will more than adequately equip you to manage most of the day-to-day issues you will encounter.
2. *The transition takes planning*. Moving from where you are to starting a new business needs careful thought. There are

separate elements to this process: you need to manage your job exit professionally; you need to find a great business idea and work through a solid start up plan.

3 *Keeping it simple.* If there is one phrase we would use to sum up our own organisation, it would be "simple and focused". We are convinced that this was a primary reason we were successful. We cannot encourage you strongly enough to adopt this philosophy for your business. It really helps you become very good at your core activity, and it is such excellence that will be the cornerstone of your successful company.

4 *It is the best of both worlds.* The distance between a small and large company can be much smaller than you may think. SMEs have some inherent advantages over a traditional corporate. They are nimble, quick, flexible and non bureaucratic. Conversely, the big corporate will typically exude professionalism and have broader resources, both financial and depth of people skills. As a former employee, you have the opportunity and ability to maintain and present a professional front whilst enjoying the benefits of the SME structure. It is the best of both worlds.

5 *Enjoy it.* Above all, it should be about enjoying your work life more. You can do things your way, work to the values that you believe in and interweave your business and personal lives to your own agenda. You are the boss and the buck stops with you, but you will find that fulfilling and satisfying, even when the going gets tough.

Whilst we enjoyed significant growth and some financial success, it is nevertheless the lifestyle factors that dominate our thinking when we reflect on why we enjoyed being entrepreneurs so much.

There are lots of things to get right if you decide to pack in the day job and start a business. We hope we have conveyed that if you apply your experiences properly it is a lot simpler than you might think to make it a success. The opportunity to create your own style of operation brings many benefits and huge personal satisfaction. Give it some thought – it may just be for you!

And finally...

Our reflections

As part of our preparation before writing this book, we reflected back on our life as owner managers of Ubevco and produced a list of the things we liked best about the experience.

We did it independently but the results were largely the same:

1. *Camaraderie*. There was a real team ethic and it really felt everyone was on the same side and working towards the same goals. Much more so than any other job we had. It still exists even after people have moved on. If anything, this is what we miss.
2. *No investors to keep happy*. Not having to spend lots of unproductive time explaining, reporting and managing external investors was a joy, notwithstanding the occasional need to talk to the bank manager.
3. *Financial reward*. We were fortunate to earn excellent financial rewards that secured our retirement. But even in the early days when our finances were tight and we were earning modestly, the knowledge that we had generated the income ourselves was in itself rewarding.
4. *Friendships*. Great friendships have come from every area of our business. We formed some long-term business relationships that have developed into lasting friendships stretching from Mexico to Singapore, South Africa to Australia. Closer to home, we worked with great people who offered us no end of support along the way as only friends can. And we are delighted that six of our employees who met whilst working for us eventually married.
5. *The ten-minute journey to work*. We have laboured this one a lot in this book – just goes to show how important it was to us!
6. *Developing others*. We take pride in seeing how well our people have subsequently prospered in their careers after a business grounding at Ubevco.

7 *Our brands were successful.* The majority of brands we had the pleasure of managing left us in better health than when they arrived.

8 *The parties.* Well they were called "company conferences" but this was where we built the culture and where we saw it displayed. We still talk about them. Most of the examples that we could use to explain this are not publishable in a book!

9 *We hope we were good bosses.* We tried to be open, honest and fair and whilst we doubt that everyone we dealt with or employed loved us completely, we do believe that for the most part they knew we were doing our best.

10 *Having the final word!*

Bibliography

New business ideas:

Bragg, A. and Bragg, M. (2005) *Developing New Business Ideas A Step by Step Guide to Creating New Business Ideas Worth Backing*, FT Publishing.

—(2010) *"The HBR List. Breakthrough Ideas for 2010"*, *Harvard Business Review.*

Marketing:

Hammond, J. (2008) *Branding Your Business: Promoting Your Business, Attracting Customers and Standing out in the Marketplace*, Kogan Page.

Norman, J. (2004) *What No-One Ever Tells You about Marketing Your Own Business, Real Life Marketing Advice from 101 Successful Entrepreneurs*, Kaplan Business.

Business plan:

Mullins, J. (2010) *The New Business Road Test: What Entrepreneurs and Executives Should Do before Writing a Business Plan*, FT Publishing.

Culture:

Covey, S. (2004) *The Seven Habits of Highly Effective People*, Franklin Covey.

People management:

Newell Brown, J. (2011) *The Complete Guide to Recruitment A Step by Step Approach to Selecting, Assessing and Hiring the Right People*, Kogan Page.

Yeung, R. (2010) *The Sunday Times Successful Interviewing and Recruitment*, Kogan Page.

Grout, J. and Perrin, S. (2005) *Recruiting Excellence: an Insider's Guide to Sourcing Top Talent*, McGraw-Hill.

Managing growth:

Duncan, L. (2012) *Double Your Business: How to Break through the Barriers to Higher Growth, Turnover and Profit*, FT Publishing.

Change management:

Hayes, J. (2010) *The Theory and Practice of Change Management*, Palgrave Macmillan.

Kotter, J. (2006) *Our Iceberg Is Melting*, Macmillan.

Index